How to Work With a Secretary

The Boss's Handbook

Teresa Torres

Annabell Publishing
Denver, Colorado

How To Work With a Secretary

The Boss's Handbook

All rights reserved.
Copyright © 2004 Annabell Publishing.

No part of this book may be reproduced or transmitted in any form or by any means, electronic or mechanical, including photocopying, recording, or by an information storage and retrieval system, except by a reviewer who may quote brief passages in a review to be printed in a magazine or newspaper, without permission in writing from the publisher. For information contact Annabell Publishing, P.O. Box 22754, Denver, Colorado 80222-0754.
First printing 2004.

ISBN 0-9655608-1-3
Library of Congress Catalog Number
2001126492

Manufactured in the United States of America.

TABLE OF CONTENTS

	Introduction	v
1	What Is a Secretary?	1
2	Why Women Make the Best Secretaries	5
3	The Different Levels of Secretaries	8
4	The Boss's Working Relationship With the Secretary	12
	Praise	13
	Respect	14
	Communicate	16
	Listen	20
	Converse	22
	Humor	22
	Honor	24
	Power	24
	Criticism	26
	Faultfinding	26
	Problems	29
	Profanity	30
	Sexual Harassment	30
	Feedback	32
	Mission Statement	32
5	The Daily Work Routine	33
6	The Weekly Meeting With Your Secretary	38
	How to Conduct the Weekly Meeting	40
7	How to Present Assignments to Your Secretary	43
8	Coordinating Calendars and Event Planning	48
	Calendars	48
	Event Planning	52

9	**How to Use a Microcassette for Dictation**	**55**
	The Dictation Process	56
	Summary of Dictation Rules	58
10	**The Forces Behind Producing a Document**	**59**
11	**Maintaining Standard Operating Procedures**	**64**
	The Filing System	65
	Telephone Protocols	67
	Greeting Visitors	70
	Processing Mail	71
	Email Processing and Protocols	74
	Correspondence Standards	77
	Scenario for Producing a Document	78
	Procedures for Meetings	82
	Preparing Meeting Minutes	84
12	**The Boss's Working Relationship With Other Office Personnel**	**86**
13	**Finding the Right Secretary**	**90**
	Secretarial Pay Scale	90
	Matching Personalities	96
	The Hiring Edge	100
14	**How to Work With a New Secretary**	**102**
15	**Ergonomics and the Secretary's Health**	**107**
16	**Supervising the Secretary**	**112**
17	**The Performance Review**	**115**
	Index	118

INTRODUCTION

It is the dilemma of our day that colleges do not teach courses on how to work with a secretary. There are all kinds of printed matter available for secretaries on how to do their job. There are one-day seminars designed to teach administrative assistants how to be the best at their job. Unfortunately, these things only address half of the boss-secretary team and basically become ineffective with a boss that does not know how to properly work with a secretary.

Just as there are standards and procedures set for record keeping, so there are standards, procedures, and protocols that have been established for the boss-secretary relationship. Bosses are not born knowing how to work with their secretary. Their college education did not prepare them on how to develop this relationship. Although they may have been prepared to be a leader, being the lead in the boss-secretary team is altogether different. The difference lies in the personal aspect of their close working relationship.

The full spectrum of responsibilities that the boss has toward the secretary is far greater than most bosses realize. Just as the book, *A Christmas Carol,* teaches the god-given responsibilities an employer has toward its employees, so it is the same with this relationship. Developing a harmonious working relationship with the secretary is the absolute responsibility of the boss—because the boss is the lead.

Any boss-secretary team can be turned into a harmonious working relationship, which is the ultimate goal of this book. Following the standards, procedures, and protocols set forth in this book will be a step in the right direction. A willingness to learn and to improve oneself will go a long way towards improving the working relationship. The difference in the boss-secretary relationship begins with you—the boss. And may it begin here with this book and be an ongoing process thereafter.

*Thanks be to God
for the inspiration
in writing this book.*

1

What Is a Secretary?

When you think of the word secretary, does the image of typist come to mind? Let's correct this image and put it into perspective. A secretary is an assistant. She is the boss's advisor, business partner, and confidante. A doctor is a profession, a lawyer is a profession, a secretary is a profession. This should put it into perspective. Your profession and the secretarial profession are codependent.

Both the boss and the secretary take ownership of the work that is produced in the boss's name, thus becoming a partnership. A partnership is a team of two or more that work together toward a common goal. As an assistant to the boss, the secretary conducts a wide range of duties that support the boss's position. Besides clerical duties, much of the secretarial position relies on attitude and personal attributes.

In general terms the secretary is responsible for taking care of the boss. In all aspects of the word, she becomes your assistant. She constantly spends her time responding to your needs and the needs of others in achieving common goals. Functionally, a secretary is an assistant that conducts record keeping and document producing duties, and coordinates activities. She is also responsible for keeping track of you. Your calendar is an important aspect of this responsibility. Your secretary is your liaison with the business community and with company personnel. If you are an executive level manager, they should go through her to contact you. Your secretary represents you wherever she goes. She is an extension of you. Your secretary is your advocate, your defender, and your right arm. This is the essence of what a secretary is and a clue to the type of working relationship that should exist between the boss and the secretary.

The basic functional duties of a secretary can consist of typing, filing, answering phones, processing mail, and using a computer and other office and business equipment. Office and business equipment can consist of a manual typewriter, memory typewriter, desktop computer, laptop computer, telephone answering system, telephone switchboard, cellular phone, answer machine, voice mail systems, postage metering machines, photocopy machines, facsimile machines, paper folding machines, binding machines, laminating machines, dictation machines, dictation transcription machines, microcassettes, cassette copying machines, printers, scanners, projectors, CD copying machines, pagers, alpha-pagers, short-wave radios, time clocks, etc.

The use of a computer goes far beyond the ability of being able to use a keyboard such as you would a typewriter. It is the working knowledge and ability to productively use software programs such as word processors, spreadsheets, databases, web browsers, email access programs, presentation programs, accounting/bookkeeping programs, and desktop publishing programs. The skill level in which the software is used is directly related to the level of secretary that is employed.

A secretary's attributes entail a large variety of personality traits that are typically used in secretarial positions. Some of them can be put into categories. People skills are one of the most prominent and include such things as being a team player, communication skills, motivating people, being able to handle people of all dispositions, being able to work well with a wide variety of nationalities, and basically being people oriented. The highest paid attribute is organizational skills. Following in hot pursuit are confidentiality and attention to detail. Management type skills that are commonly found in administrative level secretarial positions include being a self-starter, decision maker, problem solver, being goal oriented, and having a take-charge personality.

Another dimension to a secretary is her knowledge and ability to conduct herself in a professional manner according to office etiquette. Office etiquette not only includes the proper way to greet visitors and answer phones, it is following the established protocols for filing and producing documents such as correspondence, memorandums, agendas, meeting minutes, reports, and presentations. How the boss is represented verbally and how the boss looks on paper make a lasting impression. This is a crucial responsibility of the secretary.

As if all of these skills and attributes weren't enough, your secretary is expected to be a master of the English language. Spelling, punctuation, and grammar are supposed to be her forte. There is a lot your secretary needs to know in the office environment in order to function in a responsible and productive manner. Knowing how to work with a secretary professionally is essential to your success, no matter what the size of your office.

2

Why Women Make the Best Secretaries

The majority of secretaries are women. For generations women have been secretaries. Formal secretarial education began in the eighteenth century in the United States as the need for bookkeeping and stenography was created by the Industrial Revolution. This evolved into a standardized set of procedures for all aspects of the office including regulations for filing. Before the dictation machine notes were taken by hand with cryptical symbols known as shorthand. These office procedures and duties required attributes that women naturally had, therefore secretarial positions were filled by women. There is a perfectly logical and scientific reason for this.

A woman's brain functions differently than a man's in ways that cause her to develop the attributes a secretary needs. A secretary needs to be thinking of a multitude of items at the same time. This process of thinking can be compared to a computer. If her brain were a computer, it would have a larger random access memory (RAM). For example, as the secretary is transcribing a letter that the boss wrote, it mentions an issue that she saw in a memo that she filed two weeks ago in a completely unrelated file. At the same time she is connecting several emails she has reviewed that made mention of the same issue. Her mind is simultaneously connecting the authors of the emails with the author of the memo, with the addressee of the letter, and all of the pertinent facts. As the secretary continues to transcribe the letter, her multifaceted mind continues to connect the information she is assimilating with all possible scenarios. Then the secretary is able to advise the boss of these connections. There is a scientific explanation for this. When a woman's brain is activated, there is a wide spread of neuron activity which crosses between the right side of the brain and the left side which produces a spectrum of connectivity. Men's brains don't send out as many neurons when activated, so they tend to stay more intently focused on a singular subject matter.

Women verbalize more than men do from the day they are born. This gives women the opportunity to increase their vocabulary and use their language skills more often. This difference is also caused by neuron activity in the brain. With the basis of a secretary's job in document production, which relies heavily on her ability to use the English language, this becomes a major attribute.

The most significant reason women make better secretaries is because they are emotionally based. This emotional base provides two prominent attributes. The first pertains to their memory. Since most women automatically attach emotions to their experiences, and experiences with emotions are remembered for a longer period of time, their memories are sharper. Sharp memories for secretaries formulate into attention to detail and organizational skills, among others. These primary attributes make for an excellent secretary.

A woman's emotional base is derived from the right brain being used more often than the left. When this is connected with an injection of neuron activity, it creates an emotional intelligence. This special intelligence creates a "sixth" sense. This is how a woman "just knows" about certain things. This is also called a woman's intuition and can be interpreted as the leverage of a secretary's people skills. A woman with a keen sense of intuition makes an exceptional secretary.

The way a woman's brain functions differs from that of a man. This is not to say that men don't have the same attributes. It only signifies that women prominently display these abilities far more often and more naturally; therefore, more women become secretaries.

3

The Different Levels of Secretaries

Our society has put a negative stigma on the title of secretary. To elevate the title and put its true description in place, it has been upgraded to assistant. It is socially proper to refer to your secretary as your assistant instead of "just a secretary." The levels of secretaries can be divided into three basic secretarial titles: secretary, assistant, and administrative assistant. Even though the title of secretary is still used today, the duties it carries usually fall into the mid to lower range, as well as the salary. Assistants are considered to be a higher level of secretary, with salaries larger than that of the basic secretarial title. An executive level secretary carries the title of administrative assistant or a similar derivative and is the highest paid.

Titles that have fallen by the wayside include typist and word processor. This is logical, for if a person can type or

Chapter 3 The Different Levels of Secretaries

use a word processor, then she can also file and answer phones—which are the basics for the secretarial title.

Education plays a roll in the secretarial titles. Although experience and education are usually considered synonymous in the secretarial realm, it is a combination of college and experience that is the most commonly expected for administrative titles. Education for the basic secretarial titles usually requires a high school diploma. There is a national examination for secretaries that awards the rating of CPS (Certified Professional Secretary) through universities and colleges. This rating permits the secretary to place the rating of CPS after her name. As can be expected, only the highest level of secretaries would have this rating. The level of education or years of experience are directly related to the proper usage of the English language. Grammar and punctuation are reflected in all printed matter. Producing documents, which are printed matter, is a major portion of the secretarial duties. Being in command of the English language is a crucial aspect for secretarial positions and is also reflected in the different levels of secretaries.

To further define the levels of secretaries, the most popularly used titles in the United States can be divided into five titles that correspond directly to their pay scale. They are: administrative assistant, executive secretary, administrative secretary, secretary, and secretary/receptionist. Although there are variations of these titles, these are the most commonly used. A general description of these titles and salary ranges follow. The salary ranges are dependent upon the area in which the position is located.

Administrative Assistant
Salary range: $20,000 - $65,000
Attributes: Organizational and communication skills, self-starter and team player, "can do" attitude, confidentiality
Skills: Word processing, spreadsheet, and presentation programs; event planning and scheduling; financial/accounting abilities

This title also deals with various levels of confidentiality. The finance/accounting capabilities are not that of a full-time accountant or bookkeeper, rather it is the ability to perform light accounting and financial tasks, and to review financial reports.

Executive Secretary
Salary range: $30,000 - $60,000
Attributes: Organizational and communication skills, self-starter and team player, "can do" attitude, confidentiality
Skills: Word processing, spreadsheet, and presentation programs; event planning and scheduling; financial/accounting abilities

This title usually supports one executive level manager. Confidentiality is the key attribute.

Administrative Secretary
Salary range: $20,000 - $45,000
Attributes: Organizational and communication skills, self-starter and team player, "can do" attitude
Skills: Word processing, spreadsheet, and presentation programs; scheduling and math abilities

This title is geared toward document production, especially with reports, proposals, transcription, and correspondence composition.

Secretary
Salary range: $15,000 - $40,000
Attributes: Positive attitude, interpersonal skills, quick-learner
Skills: Word processing programs and scheduling
The skills are more important than the attributes in this title. There is usually a heavy amount of document production and answering a main phone line.

Secretary / Receptionist
Salary range: $13,000 - $30,000
Attributes: Positive attitude, interpersonal skills, quick-learner
Skills: Telephone answering systems and word processing programs
As the double-title indicates, the duties are divided into basic secretarial and answering the phones. The main duty of answering the telephone, usually a main incoming line, is the primary focus in this title.

4

The Boss's Working Relationship With the Secretary

Having a successful working relationship is vital in any working environment. Success is defined as a union in harmony. As human beings in the working class, we spend more of our waking hours in a work environment than anywhere else. We develop working relationships with the people we work with. These working relationships affect our daily lives. Because of the close interaction between the boss and the secretary, the development of a harmonious working relationship is crucial, not only to the success of the business, but also in each other's personal lives.

As the supervisor of the secretary, the boss is directly responsible for guiding the course taken to build the working relationship. Tools are needed for building. Nothing is created, made, or built without tools. The tools used for building working relationships are derived from the psychological composition of the boss. The tools necessary to build a harmonious working relationship include: praise, respect, humor, honor, communication, trust, listening, feedback, a mission statement, and a personal interest in each other's well being. How are these tools used?

Working relationships are built using the tools through goals. Goals guide the working relationship in certain directions. Not using these tools or the improper use of them can cause the working relationship to go in a negative direction. The overall goal that the boss should aim for is a secretary that is loyal, trustworthy, and dedicated. This equates to a harmonious working relationship that results in a secretary that is highly productive—which is the epitome of this relationship. Unless the overall goal is earnestly and diligently strived for, it will not be achieved.

The boss needs to be thoroughly acquainted with the duties and responsibilities of the secretary. It is the foundation upon which the working relationship is built. In understanding how each responsibility should be accomplished, the boss will be able to effectively use the tools. It is the basis with which to give praise, show true admiration and respect, find humor, gain trust, share information about, and discuss. The boss needs to earnestly develop a workable personal version of these tools and then use them toward achieving the goal of a harmonious working relationship with the secretary. Commitment to achieving the goal is the key to successfully obtaining it.

Praise

The boss's working relationship with the secretary is like a bank account. Deposits are made by giving her praise and compliments, saying kind words to her, and doing kind

13

things for her. Withdrawals take place when you are curt with her, say unkind words to her, forget to inform her of your schedule, or in any way show negativity towards her. Withdrawals are also made when you ask her to stay late, expect her to do an assignment in which she has to take work home with her, or ask her to go the extra mile for you. Without sufficient funds in a bank account, you cannot make a withdrawal. Doing so will cause an overdraft, your account will be in the red, and your relationship in the negative. A substantial withdrawal takes place when constructive criticism is given, when reproving or reprimanding. Bank accounts earn interest and so does this account with your secretary. Interest will compound daily as she goes to bat for you in unheralded arenas, especially in the battle zone of the office. If you have not established this account with your secretary, it is advisable to do so. You can only benefit from it–it's a win-win situation.

Praise is the verbal expression of approval and appreciation. It is a basic building block in any relationship–especially this one. It is an investment with benefits that reach far into the future. Praise must be given every day. Keep this proverb in mind: *A compliment today will help weather life's storms tomorrow.*

Respect

In a nutshell, respect is the process whereby we think highly of other things, especially another person, and show consideration towards it. Our mannerisms display what we feel and how we think. We can look upon someone with respect that reflects our sentiments of esteem. Respect is shown through thoughtful acts of concern and kindness. Respect is also reflected in the manner in which we speak

Chapter 4   The Boss's Working Relationship With the Secretary

PRAISE

A compliment today will help weather life's storms tomorrow.

to one another. How we address each other when we are conversing, or at any time, can show respect. It is a continuum for a respectful relationship. The use of titles when calling upon each other is important in developing and maintaining respect. Sadly, this formality has been lost today. The common usage of first names allows familiarity in the working relationship and destroys the foundation for respect and the credibility of the person. When no academic title is available, the established titles of Mr., Mrs., Ms., or Miss should be used. Respect goes in both directions; titles should be used for both the boss and the secretary. This means that the boss should address the secretary with a title at all times and vice versa. Here's another proverb: *Formality builds respect–familiarity destroys it.*

Communicate

Sharing information is communication. It is exchanging thoughts, ideas, feelings, and information. It is a transmission of data from one person to another. Information can be shared verbally or through the written word. Mind reading is not an acceptable form of communication. Sharing information is the road map the secretary uses to support the boss's position, which is what she was hired to do. It is your responsibility to provide the secretary with the necessary information she needs to do her job. In return, it is the secretary's responsibility to keep you informed. *Communication is a two-way street.*

There are a variety of devices available that provide a means with which to communicate. These devices consist of a telephone, cellular phone, answer machine, voice mail, and pager. In an effort to utilize the communication devices to the fullest, they should be prioritized to establish a level

Chapter 4 The Boss's Working Relationship With the Secretary

RESPECT

Formality builds respect - familiarity destroys it.

of importance as a code in contacting each other. For example, the boss carries a cellular phone and a pager but does not always respond to them. The cellular phone is ignored during meetings and important conversations. The pager is viewed when messages are received, and return calls are made when convenient. The order of priority for the secretary to contact the boss would be to use the pager first. If the boss does not respond within a few minutes, then use the cellular phone. The boss's responsibility in establishing this priority system would be to always view the pager message and respond immediately if it is from the secretary. Of course, it is expected that the secretary would use discretion with the priority system. Many times the item of concern can wait until the boss returns to the office. With this type of priority system and the variety of communication devices available, there is no excuse for the boss and the secretary to be out of contact with each other. Sharing vital information as it is needed is essential in any business.

The computer provides another avenue with which to transmit information. With it we access word processing and email programs. Sometimes the written word is the best method to relay information. Writing instructions are an excellent way of documenting them, as well as keeping track of them. There are times when memos and emails are the best way to share information. Sometimes handwritten messages on message pads or sticky notes suit the purpose.

The ability to communicate effectively between one another and the manner in which it is carried out is a very visible part of your working relationship with your secretary. Anyone that comes into contact with your team is made aware of it; therefore, the better you communicate with each other, the better you are going to look. Whatever

Chapter 4 The Boss's Working Relationship With the Secretary

COMMUNICATE

The more informed your secretary is, the more committed she'll be.

means or devices are used, information should be flowing back and forth between the boss and the secretary constantly. If there are confidential issues to be considered, remember that your secretary is your confidante. Confidentiality does not mean that you keep secrets from each other. A lack of communication will erode a working relationship. A good rule of thumb in knowing what to communicate can be summed up with this proverb: *The more informed your secretary is, the more committed she'll be.*

Listen

Listening is an art. It is a principle that must be learned. It is a discipline that affects our behavior. Listening takes more than just ears; it takes a receptive mind and an intuitive heart. It is reading between the lines. Learn to discern what is being meant through the mechanism of what is being said. The tone of voice, inflections of speech, and the words chosen all combine together to formulate the true meaning of what is spoken.

Listening also takes paying attention to body language. The way our body is positioned and the many gestures that are made during a conversation reveal much about what we are feeling and is a clue to interpreting the true meaning of what is being said. For example, crossed arms are an indication of defense and rejection; it can be a negative action. Open arms can signify readiness or acceptance.

Taking into consideration the purpose of the verbiage is also an important aspect of listening. This is perhaps where listening and hearing become separated. You can spend a lifetime listening and never hear a word. *To hear is to perceive the spoken word, while listening is the act of paying attention to it. Listen for the purpose of hearing.*

Chapter 4 The Boss's Working Relationship With the Secretary

LISTEN

To hear is to perceive the spoken word, while listening is the act of paying attention to it. Listen for the purpose of hearing.

Converse

It is inevitable that there will be a personal side to the working relationship between the boss and the secretary. This personal side balances out a well developed working relationship. Taking an interest in each other's personal lives instills the bond of loyalty, which translates into dedication. The boss should take a few minutes every day to converse with the secretary. This means to talk informally about nonwork related subjects. Discuss a current event in the news, what is happening in your family life, the show you watched on television last night, what you did over the weekend, the weather, and other such trivial things. Also project an interest in her views and opinions–it shows her that you care. Conversing and becoming personally involved in each other's lives are two different things. Keep your conversing cordially proper. The effect of this relationship building tool is summarized with this proverb: *She can't care about the work she does for you until you show how much you care about her.*

Humor

What working environment doesn't need comic relief every now and then. The seriousness of the work you produce can weigh heavily on the mind. An injection of humor can go a long way to lighten the intensity of it. Having a sense of humor is a personality trait that not everyone has–for some it must be learned. Learn to react with humor at mistakes or when something goes wrong. Humor can bring a positive light into a negative situation. It helps to lighten an overwhelming project.

Humor is light heartedness and never should be mis-

Chapter 4 The Boss's Working Relationship With the Secretary

CONVERSE

She can't care about the work she does for you until you show how much you care about her.

taken for practical jokes or jokes of any kind. Jokes are deliberately made to provoke laughter at the expense of others or with subject matters that are off color. Humor does not cause laughter; rather, it induces a smile and a chuckle or two. *Humor is a ray of sunshine on a hectic day.*

What do you do when you find a typographical error in a publication that just came back from the printer and had been proofed by three different secretaries and two bosses? Take it with a grain of salt, add a touch of humor, and chalk it up to Murphy's law.

Honor

Honoring the secretary on specific days is an absolute must that etiquette dictates in the working relationship between the boss and the secretary. These dates are her birthday, Secretary's Day, and Christmas. It is appropriate to buy her a floral arrangement on Secretary's Day and optional to also take her to lunch. You should always buy her a gift for Christmas. For her birthday a gift or floral arrangement is acceptable. Never forget these dates. Honor is a form of respect. To forget to honor your secretary on these special days shows disrespect.

Power

Depending on the level of boss you are, your secretary carries the weight of that power. Secretaries, especially administrative level secretaries, are "power" positions. Remember that your secretary is an extension of you. She has the authority to act on your behalf. The greater aspect of the power she holds is within the working relationship. Because she works closely with you, she has the power to

CRITICISM

Never criticize! Encourage improvement in a constructive, kind, and meaningful manner.

influence you substantially; therefore, building and maintaining trust is an imperative.

Criticism

The negative connotation associated with the word criticism has been aptly earned. It is judging a fault to the point of condemnation. When we are criticized it is the act of passing judgment. We are made to feel guilty. Our self-esteem and self-worth are lost. We want to crawl into a hole and hide.

What purpose does criticism serve if it makes a person feel so bad? None. If improvement is needed, it must be dealt with in a constructive manner. If you cannot do so constructively, then don't do it! The improvement needed should never be addressed with an attitude of disapproval or anger. Never speak to your secretary in an autocratic, sarcastic, or condescending tone of voice. The most productive way to encouragae improvement is to show, in a helpful and meaningful manner, the improvement that you would like to see achieved. To summarize: *Never criticize! Encourage improvement in a constructive, kind, and meaningful manner.*

Faultfinding

Faultfinding is a negative way of thinking. It is destructive to the working relationship. Faultfinding is the practice of finding someone to blame for a fault. Always pointing the finger at someone for mistakes, errors, and things gone wrong. The attitude of having to blame someone for faults will slow down the work flow between the boss and the secretary.

Chapter 4   The Boss's Working Relationship With the Secretary

PROBLEMS

To change
a situation
one must first
change oneself.

Errors and mistakes are ever present, especially in an age where data is quickly transmitted electronically, and the day is filled with constant interruptions and a rush to meet deadlines. As human beings we are all imperfect. Your attitude and approach with your secretary should be one devoid of blame. This is an imperfect world populated with imperfect human beings. Faultfinding is a destructive act.

Problems

Your relationship with your secretary should never deteriorate to the point that you "have words" with each other. As the boss you are expected to be a leader. A respected leader does not stoop to such lows. It is your responsibility to guide the working relationship through all obstacles with an even temper, nonthreatening mannerisms, and an intellectually understanding mind.

Never say anything negative about your secretary publicly. It makes you look bad. If there are conflicts that arise between the two of you that remain unresolved, seek advice from the proper authority that is dictated by company policy. If no company policy exists on the subject, your boss or the human resources department is your best resource. Never end the day without resolving conflicts. Unresolved conflicts have a way of festering overnight and brewing over days and becoming mountains of harsh feelings that will be emitted in unconscious ways that others will pick up on. Again, this makes the boss look bad.

Problems arise when the boss is not properly using the tools necessary for building a harmonious working relationship. The boss should review the tools and conduct a self-evaluation of their usage. It would be wise for the boss to

Chapter 4 The Boss's Working Relationship With the Secretary

PROFANITY

Profanity
has no place
in the work place.

keep in mind this proverb: *To change a situation one must first change oneself.*

Profanity

Profanity has no place in the work place–no matter who you are, what title you may have, or what the situation may be. There are no excuses or exceptions here.

Sexual Harassment

Sexual harassment is any conduct or behavior that can be construed as sexual in nature, whether perpetrated by individuals of different sexes or the same sex. It is any conduct of a sexual nature that is made explicitly or implicitly as a term or condition of a person's employment or interferes with a person's work or working conditions. Sexual harassment is also sexual advances, whether for sexual favors in exchange for employment benefits or threats of reprisals if sexual favors are not given. It is prohibited by federal and state laws. It is impossible to define all the aspects and interpretations of sexual harassment. Nevertheless, the basics can be divided into four categories: verbal, written, visual, and physical.

Verbal

Offensive or unwelcome remarks, jokes, or noises; derogatory comments or slurs; graphic words used to describe the body or the way a person is dressed; requests for sexual favors; name calling or degrading language of any kind; and verbal references toward a person's sexual practices.

Chapter 4 The Boss's Working Relationship With the Secretary

Written

Anything written on paper or electronically via the Internet or email, etc., that is graphic or degrading that describes the body or the way a person is dressed or refers to a person's sexual practices; suggestive or obscene letters, memos, notes, or invitations; and unwelcome love letters.

Visual

Displaying in any manner including electronic transmition via the Internet or email matter that is sexual in nature, such as photographs, drawings, paintings, pictures, etc., or material of any kind in any format; e.g., calendars, postcards, magazines, greeting cards, wall hangings, etc. Sexual in nature is described as offensive or obscene exposure of parts of the body, suggestive poses, and pornography. Staring at certain parts of a person's body, sexually-oriented gestures, and suggestively exposing parts of the body is also construed as sexual harassment.

Physical

Physical contact such as touching, back rubbing, patting, pinching, grabbing, poking, or brushing against; impeding or blocking movement; interference with a person's work; and assault.

The working relationship with the secretary should be devoid of anything that could be construed as sexual harassment. Some points to consider incorporating into your working relationship would be to never touch unless it's a professional handshake, always speak to your secretary with respect, and treat your secretary in an honorable manner.

Feedback

Feedback is an excellent tool with which to gauge the success of the boss-secretary team. Feedback is a means of receiving a partial return of information that was sent out; it can be returned in the form of a reaction or response. Once the feedback is received, it is what is done with it that makes it a useful tool. The most productive uses are to analyze a situation and to evaluate it for the purpose of improvement.

Whether the boss realizes it or not, feedback is continually being returned; this is where listening skills are honed. Learn to be perceptive to feedback and to incorporate it into the working relationship with your secretary.

Mission Statement

Establish a mission statement for the working relationship with your secretary–for together you make a team. A mission statement is a goal that summarizes how you want others to view your team. The statement should be short and concise so that it will be easy to remember. It should inspire a sense of purpose and unity and help dispel the singularity of independent agendas. Have your mission statement printed and posted where it can be viewed every day; then strive to follow it.

5

The Daily Work Routine

As simple as it may sound, the boss should begin each day with a pleasant, uplifting greeting to the secretary. This sets the tone of your working relationship with her for the whole day. An occasional smile and encouraging words and praises throughout the day will go a long way toward getting the job done. Your secretary spends her time serving you and others in a thankless profession within the battle zone of the interior office. She has to deal with all kinds of negativity in the form of gossip, rivalry, backbiting, and resentment that go on in the office which the boss knows nothing about. Your kind attentions can truly make the work flow more smoothly.

As the new day begins, your secretary should have some basic primary tools at her fingertips. The boss's schedule for the day should be easily accessible, and her "to-do" list with priorities indicated should be within sight. You may opt to begin each day with a short discussion of your separate to-do lists. This will help to synchronize your common goals and keep the lines of communication open.

The secretary should spend the first half hour retrieving her voice mail messages and reviewing emails. Depending on the level of secretary and her specific job duties, she may also be doing the same on your behalf. This time period is also used to return calls and respond to email messages. If you use a tickler file system, it should be checked and any items for the day placed in your in-basket.

When the mail arrives it should be processed within a reasonable length of time. Mail is a virtual means of communication that requires a concerted effort in keeping it up. Although your secretary can easily get caught up in heavy document production, she should always take time out to process the mail on a daily basis.

The out-basket should be checked several times a day. The out-basket is normally located in the boss's office, usually on the desk. It is the means by which paperwork is transferred from your desk to your secretary's. The paperwork you place in your out-basket requires some kind of action. Sticky notes with instructions for your secretary to follow should be on each item or set of items. The out-basket is the avenue by which you are giving your secretary nonverbal assignments. See Chapter 7, How to Present Assignments to Your Secretary, for further instructions on this subject.

One of your secretary's responsibilities is to keep track of you. This means that she needs to know your whereabouts when you are not in your office. It is the boss's responsibility to notify the secretary when leaving the office building. Neglecting to do so constitutes a lack of

34

communication on your part. It does not look good when your secretary has to hunt you down by making calls to other departments and places where she thinks you might be. When the "big" boss wants to know where you are, she had better have the answer. Common courtesy and respect are elements of your working relationship that need to be exercised constantly. Use these elements to make it a habit of notifying your secretary every time you leave the office. It is also absolutely essential that you let her know when you are leaving for the day. If your secretary leaves before you at the end of the day, then she should provide you with this same courtesy.

There are many facets to your secretary's job that take place on a daily basis that are autonomous. The more noticeable facets include answering the telephone, interfacing with other office personnel, greeting visitors, word processing, scheduling, and using office equipment and machines. The non-physical facets of her job are the personal attributes she uses in the working environment. These can include solving problems, motivating the boss, exercising confidentiality, coordinating, making decisions, organizing, self-motivating, quickly learning new things that come her way, communicating, and becoming a detective to locate lost paperwork and missing bosses. If you happen upon your secretary someday and she appears to be staring into open space, remember that the wheels of her mind have to turn a million miles per minute to remain focused on assisting you. There is more to being a secretary than being a word processor. Just because your secretary does not produce a document on a daily basis does not mean that she is not working. It is the boss's responsibility to thoroughly understand all aspects of the secretary's duties.

Filing is one of those duties that the secretary may find

unpleasant, but it is crucial to the operation of a well organized office. The "perfect" scenario would be that the secretary takes time every day to file. Unfortunately, this may be impossible. Due to the trend of cutting back personnel and doubling-up duties, secretaries tend to be overloaded with work, especially those that are heavy document producers.

Establish a "down-time" for your secretary to work on major projects or assignments involving a lot of detail. Interruptions cause errors. Interruptions slow down the productive time it takes to work on a project. After every interruption she must reacquaint herself with the work and rethink the process in order to continue where she left off. Telephones and visitors are the major source of interruptions. A downtime would be a period of time in which she would be able to work free from interruptions. This would mean that the phones would not be answered and visitors would not be accepted. A daily downtime is recommended for a secretary in a fast-paced heavy document production environment. A periodic downtime is recommended for catching up on the workflow, and a special downtime is recommended for those major projects. Consider providing a regularly scheduled downtime for your secretary.

No assignment should be given to your secretary within the last hour of the day. If you are preparing a project for her, wait until the morning of the next day to present it. Assignments toward the end of the day tend to cause undue pressure and concern as she works it through her mind how she's going to fit it into her workflow. Only emergencies should be considered with the true nature of the emergency being evaluated. Does it really have to be done before she goes home? Why is there an emergency? Is the emergency due to a lack of organizing your workflow?

At the end of the day your secretary should spend the

last 15-20 minutes preparing for the next working day. During this time period she should print out the boss's calendar for the next day, prepare materials for meetings the next day, review and reevaluate her to-do list, and straighten her work area. This will help her to leave the office with a peace of mind and be more quickly productive in the morning.

6

The Weekly Meeting With Your Secretary

A weekly one-on-one meeting with your secretary is the key to communicating with her. This is not an option—it is an absolute must. Your working relationship is based upon the channel of communication that operates between both of you. Meeting at least once a week with your secretary will help to develop the commitment and loyalty you need from her in your working relationship. It is the means by which you keep her informed. You are showing her respect by caring enough about her to spend your time to involve her in your workflow, and it shows how important she is as a member of your team. Remember, the more informed she is, the more committed she'll be.

The weekly meeting is more than just a time for you to inform your secretary of your activities and workflow. It is a two-way street; it's a time for both of you to share infor-

Chapter 6   The Weekly Meeting With Your Secretary

mation. Throughout the day your secretary is constantly acquiring information that can be beneficial to you. She may also need guidance in accomplishing the assignments you have given her. Because the boss is the supervisor over the secretary, the workflow should be regularly reviewed and direction should be given depending upon the level of secretary that is employed. This weekly meeting is the perfect time to do so. It is also the best environment to receive specific feedback on items of concern.

A very important aspect of the weekly meeting is the nourishment of the social bond that has developed between you and your secretary. This part of a working relationship is overlooked far too often. How is this nourishment accomplished? The answer is simple: converse. When you begin your weekly one-on-one meeting with your secretary, take a few minutes to talk about each other's personal lives, current events, office events, and anything of personal interest that is not directly related to either of your workflows. Ask her how she is doing. It's a great way to open the conversation, then take the time to listen. This demonstrates a personal interest in her well-being. Seeking her opinions will build her self-esteem. If she knows that you care about her, she will care about the work she does for you, and that is what her job is all about. Because of the perpetual fluctuation of this social bond, it must be fed often and on a regular basis or it will die.

The weekly meeting is one of the essential tools needed in the boss-secretary working relationship. Unfortunately, too many bosses do not conduct this all important, one-on-one, weekly meeting with their secretary, and this plays a large roll in the failure of their relationship.

How to Conduct the Weekly Meeting

Step One

The weekly one-on-one meeting is usually held in the boss's office. To start off the week on the right foot, this meeting should be held first thing Monday morning. The first topic of discussion should be the personal interests and issues in each of your lives. Don't rush through this; take your time and let the conversation wean itself. You may have to guide the conversation toward work-related issues pertaining to your schedule, since that is the next subject you cover in the meeting.

Step Two

You and your secretary should have separate calendars. Many use daily planner organizer calendars. If you use an electronic calendar, your secretary should print out your schedule for the week and the month prior to the meeting. As you review your calendars, focus on the current week. Give her details about your scheduled meetings and events, and instruct her in the preparations she needs to make for them. Because you do not have a copy of her schedule, you should make a note of her planned absences from the work area and office. Your next focus should be an overview of the next few weeks. Scheduling of prospective events should be discussed and any scheduling conflicts should be resolved.

Step Three

Review the assignments you have given your secretary. You should have a list from which you are working. As you go through it, discuss the

Chapter 6   The Weekly Meeting With Your Secretary

assignments that have been completed before crossing them off. Reevaluate the projected due dates on the assignments that have not been completed and change as needed. Discuss the status of current and on-going assignments, and help her find ways to resolve any issues pertaining to them.

Step Four

Present your secretary with new assignments. Remember to record them on the assignment list. Never give her an assignment without providing a due date and giving it a priority level rating. This is the time that you would change the priority level rating on her other assignments, if it is needed.

Step Five

Review your secretary's to-do list. This should be different from her calendar and assignment list. It could include such items as phone calls she needs to make, follow up items, projects she has in the works that are separate and apart from you, and departmental or company issues on which she is working.

Step Six

Review with your secretary the projects you are working on and your to-do list. Discuss future plans and her involvement in them. Take the time to thoroughly go through the projects you are, and will be, working on together.

Step Seven

Discuss other issues pertaining to your working relationship such as office events. At this time your secretary should review the phone and email messages she answered on your behalf, and she should relate contacts and issues with office personnel that

41

would be of interest to you. Keep in mind that your secretary is your "other" pair of eyes and ears. You need to glean from her all that you can. You have shared much information with her; now she is sharing information with you. What you hear may be important to you in ways that she knows not. This is one of the places where your social bond pays off.

There is one absolute rule that you must follow that goes along with the weekly meeting with your secretary and that is you must never, under any condition, cancel or rearrange the established date and time of this meeting. Doing so destroys your credibility and damages your relationship. Keep in mind the psychological aspect and purpose of this meeting. If you cancel or rearrange it, you are letting her know that she is not important and that you don't care about her. As soon as she feels unimportant, which tells her that you don't care, she will stop caring about you, and the work she is doing for you will be affected. No matter what you say, your actions speak louder than your words. If you are out of town on a business trip, conduct the meeting via telephone. At all costs, you must keep this meeting with your secretary. Your rapport with her is at stake.

The weekly meeting with your secretary is vital to your success. The ultimate benefit is a devoted secretary that is highly productive.

7

How to Present Assignments to Your Secretary

"Assignment" is the terminology used for giving the secretary work to do. The blatantly ignorant attitude of "you just tell her what to do" does not fit into a successful boss-secretary working relationship. Bosses are a dime a dozen, but a boss that knows how to work with a secretary is a gem. It's all of the little things you do in your working relationship with your secretary that makes a difference. There is an intellectually proper way to present assignments to your secretary.

Every time you ask your secretary to do something, you are giving her an assignment. They can be given verbally or written, they can be simple one-liner instructions or major projects with multiple facets, and they can be given inadvertently through the power of suggestion. Because you are the boss, what you say has power and can always be construed as a command or, in other words, an assignment. Your words should be guarded and assignments should be well thought through before they are given.

Do not make every assignment a priority, urgent, rush, or an emergency. When does the task actually need to be completed? For example, if the mail doesn't go out untill the secretary drops it off on her way home at the end of the day, then it is not necessary to have it done by 10:00 a.m. If every assignment you give your secretary is urgent and "has to be done right away," the effect of the urgency status will wear off, then when the day comes that you really do have an emergency assignment, it will be ignored. Don't be the little boy that cried wolf.

When presenting a project to your secretary, provide a priority level status and a time frame for completion. If there is a specific completion date, and even if there isn't, ask her how long it will take to complete the project. Listen carefully to her answer. You need the time divided into two parts so that you can make an educated estimated due date. The first element of the time is the real-time. Real-time is the actual amount of time it takes to do the job. Too often we equate the know-how of a task with no time. "Oh, I know how to do that. It won't take any time at all." The reality is that it takes time to do any task, no matter how well we know how to do it. The second element of time is how the real-time relates to her workload. You need to take into consideration her other assignments and their priorities, her daily routine, and the real-time it takes to do the project when estimating a due date.

The boss should know the software programs well enough to discern the feasibility of the real-time it takes to complete a project. Keep in mind that it is a rare occasion for anyone to operate a software program without causing

Chapter 7   How to Present Assignments to Your Secretary

some kind of delay, error, loss of data, or problem of some kind or other. Because software companies rush to make new versions often, no one has the time or money to obtain a true expert operating level. In your formula for determining the time it takes to complete a project, the secretary's skill level to operate the software, and the specific features that will be used for the project should be taken into account. The level of secretary that you employ usually dictates the level of expertise with which she can operate the software programs.

The manner in which you present a project or even assign a simple task to your secretary also plays a role in the time factor. The boss should give clear and precise instructions and leave nothing to be assumed—even when instructions are repetitive. This means that you need to pay attention to the details of the assignment, and provide your secretary with the tools she needs to accomplish it. Such tools can consist of names, addresses, and phone numbers that she does not have access to; a file or original documentation that you have in your office; an electronic file that is in a directory that she cannot access; any newspaper or magazine articles or other printed matter that is referenced; and lists of any kind that may help her. Your secretary has many skills but being a detective should not be one of them. Instructions should be repeated, including a brief review of standard operating procedures, to make sure that you and your secretary are in sync. Your secretary wants to do the assignment as correctly as she can the first time around. You need to do your part to make it happen. Remember, it takes team effort to produce a document—it's not just your secretary's job. See Chapter 10, The Forces Behind Producing a Document; and Chapter 11, Maintaining Standard Operating Procedures, under Correspondence

45

Standards, for more instructions on producing documents.

Simple tasks and non-priority assignments can keep your secretary busy throughout the day. Such assignments are usually the result of processing the mail and email and in response to phone calls. They can consist of such directives as: call so-and-so and find out this, forward this to so-and-so, set up a meeting with so-and-so to discuss whatever, file this with this other document, etc. To refrain from constantly interrupting your secretary and the flow of work, these simple tasks can be given to her in either of two productive ways. You can use your out-basket, which should be located in your office, usually on your desk, with written instructions on sticky notes that are attached to the document stating the action that is needed. Periodically throughout the day your secretary should check your out-basket for these assignments. The other alternative is to meet with your secretary when you have a sufficient amount of work to give her. In this meeting she should have a sticky note pad as well as a steno pad to write notes on. As you give her specific documents that require action, she should use the sticky notes. As you give her instructions in which there is no documentation, she should make notes on the steno pad. Presenting simple assignments to your secretary using either of these methods shows her the courtesy and respect you have for her and for the work she does for you. Interrupting her for simple tasks is negative behavior. Keep your working relationship positive.

When giving assignments to your secretary, write them down, making an assignment list. As her supervisor it is your responsibility to follow up on the assignments that you have given her. This list does not have to be so extensive that it includes all of the simple tasks. The crux of simple tasks is that they should be done and forgotten. If the

Chapter 7 How to Present Assignments to Your Secretary

simple task requires a return response, then it should be listed. The assignment list should consist of the following items: date given to the secretary, a brief description or title (two to four words), and a due date. This list should be reviewed at your weekly meeting with her. This list is one of the most important tools you have to work with her. Not only is it used as a guide to her workflow, it is also used in her performance review.

With the busy schedule you have as a boss and all the things you have on your mind, it is too easy to contradict a previous request or assignment or also to present the same assignment more than once. Be sure of the assignments you present to your secretary by keeping an assignment list.

Be cautious of your manner of speech and the words you choose to use when communicating with your secretary. For she listens carefully to your every word and interprets them as assignments. She will take the initiative to follow through with the things that she thinks that you want done. This is why it is good to review the tasks she is working on.

Assignments that you give to your secretary should be done in a manner of "presenting," as opposed to "giving." To present is to offer in a formal way. The psychological aspect of offering instead of commanding is the basis of the ideology of presenting assignments and does wonders in building a harmonious working relationship with your secretary.

47

8

Coordinating Calendars and Event Planning

Calendars

A calendar is a primary tool of communication. It is the axis of your working relationship with your secretary, it keeps the secretary informed as to your activities, and it allows her to prepare all necessary items for your activities. She is able to plan her schedule and workflow around you. The boss needs to learn how to effectively use a calendar. Some bosses need to overcome the stigma of letting the secretary know their whereabouts. When the secretary doesn't have the information she needs to do her job, and her job is directly related to your calendar, then her world stops turning, for the axis is broken.

There are two types of calendars: electronic and pre-printed. In printed matter they are available in many styles

Chapter 8 Coordinating Calendars and Event Planning

and sizes. Desk calendars are good for jotting down notes when talking on the phone. The most popular style of printed calendar is the daily planner organizer. Both the boss and the secretary should use one. Several of the major companies that produce these calendars provide seminars and instructional materials for use of their products. It is highly recommended that both you and your secretary take advantage of this training. Achieving the optimum use of a daily planner organizer can increase your productivity by merely keeping you organized. It works!

Electronic calendars are essential in a fast-paced business environment. The drawback is the necessity of having a computer nearby to view it. Even though they can be printed out, the printouts are less than satisfactory. Many business executives have a laptop computer so that the calendar is available. If the electronic calendar is operated on a network, the secretary can also have immediate and continual access to the boss's calendar. This eliminates the need for a double-calendar system, which is usually the case when pre-printed calendars are used.

It is your secretary's responsibility to keep track of you; therefore, it is your secretary's responsibility to be fully aware of your calendar. Calendars are for keeping track of dates and deadlines for appointments, meetings, seminars, conferences, travel, vacations, and any event that will take you away from your office. Your secretary is your liaison with the business community and company personnel. Depending on your level of management, they should go through her to contact you. She should have the authority to set up tentative appointments. To avoid unnecessary calls, when a tentative appointment is set it should be on the basis that she will only call back if the arrangement is not acceptable to you.

49

Confusion is caused when both the boss and the secretary set appointments for the boss. If your secretary sets your appointments, then she should always be the one that sets your appointments, not you. When confronted with setting your own appointment while on the telephone, you could tactfully say, "I'll transfer you to my secretary so she can set that appointment." If it is someone that is physically present, walk that person over to your secretary and give her instructions to set the appointment. If you are away from the office when someone personally requests an appointment, have that person call your secretary. Your excuse for not setting the appointment yourself is that you do not carry your calendar with you. Inevitably, there will be times when you will set your own appointment. When this happens, you must communicate this to your secretary at the first available moment.

If the boss sets appointments instead of the secretary, then it is vital that the boss maintains an efficient routine of keeping the secretary apprised of the changes to the calendar on a daily basis.

It is the boss's responsibility to provide the secretary with the necessary criteria to set up meetings. Provide her with a list of attendees, the proposed date, time, and place for the meeting, and also the subject matter. Instruct your secretary on the preparation of the materials needed, with quantities and their due date and time. An important piece of information your secretary will need is the name and phone number of the person or persons to call to set up the meeting. Many times this is not the same as the person the meeting is with. For executives it is usually their secretary. If a rearrangement of the meeting is necessary, it is always best to go through the same individual who was contacted originally to set it up.

Chapter 8   Coordinating Calendars and Event Planning

When your secretary is contacted to include you in a multiple attendee meeting, instruct her to obtain the same criteria you provide when she is setting up a meeting on your behalf. The element that is usually overlooked is the names of the other attendees. Knowing who the other participants are usually plays an important role in the meeting. After the appointment is made, a standard operating procedure should be in place for the secretary to inform the boss that an item has been put on the calendar.

Rearranging and canceling meetings can be a nightmare for your secretary when there are multiple attendees, especially attendees with very busy schedules. Setting up meetings of this sort should have been thought through thoroughly before a date and time was set. Too often an attendee is inconsiderate of the enormous amount of time it takes to set up meetings with multiple attendees and will too easily cancel. A basic rule of thumb the boss should adhere to is to keep the meetings that are set. If a rearrangement of your calendar is necessary, bump the one-on-one appointments—except the one-on-one with your secretary. By keeping your appointments and meetings you will develop respect from your peers, as well as from the society of secretaries that come in contact with you.

At the end of every day your secretary should print out the next day's calendar, then she should gather together all the materials necessary for each meeting. If you do not have a busy calendar, then printing it out weekly would suffice. She should still prepare the materials for meetings at the day before the meeting.

Event Planning

Event planning is usually the duty of an administrative level secretary. Events can consist of such things as coordinating large meetings, company picnics, seminars, and conferences. Scheduling also falls into this category. For example, scheduling computer training sessions for company personnel; or making arrangements for out-of-town visitors, such as travel, hotel, transportation, company appointments, etc.

An important aspect of event planning is the financial accountability. This is where the administrative level secretary's math and accounting skills are used. Keeping track of who gets paid when, and how, is half of the planning process. If you are working in a corporate environment, your secretary should be able to process all of the accounting vouchers in a timely manner so that the vendors get paid before the due date. She should also develop a respectful relationship with all of your vendors.

In order to plan an event your secretary needs information from you. She has many attributes, being a detective and a mind reader should not be two of them. Although it is always assumed, the why or purpose of the event should be reiterated throughout the planning stages. This will help to keep the theme flowing smoothly throughout all aspects of the event. Loosing focus of the theme is easy to do.

After establishing the why of the event, she needs to know who all of the participants will be. If the event is a large meeting, providing sufficient contact information is the boss's responsibility. If the event involves company personnel, then an updated list, either electronic or paper, is needed. If the event is a seminar or conference that your company is sponsoring for its customers, then you need to

Chapter 8 Coordinating Calendars and Event Planning

provide continual guidance in the preparation of flyers and advertisements.

This leads to the next element: how to make participant contact. The boss may decide to leave this up to the secretary's discretion, depending on the event. This does not take away your responsibility to provide her with the information she needs to do the job. No matter the process used to contact participants, you should monitor its progress. Do not do so in the manner of a micromanager; do so with a desire-to-be-informed attitude. This lets your secretary know that you care about her and the assignment. She needs to know that you care.

Sometimes the "where" of an event can be the most painstaking area of putting it together. Once again, your direction in this area is expected up front. Never assume that either of you know where the event will take place. Be thorough in giving your secretary all the information she needs to plan the event, even if it is redundant. Much time can be spent in finding the right place at the right time.

Setting a date and time is important to the success of the event. Finding that right date and time takes insight into the background of the project and sometimes a little intuition on your secretary's part. The boss should present the assignment with projected dates and times but be open to the reality that they are just that, projected.

There are many details involved in event planning; overlooking one of them can cause a domino effect and destroy the credibility of the entire event. There are products available on the market that have been designed to help with this. The most commonly used are the specifically designed pages for daily planner organizer calendars. These pages have different names depending upon the company that makes them, and they have a variety of styles from which to choose. Both the boss and the secretary should consider using products of this nature for their event planning.

Planning an event is very time consuming, which is clear to see why when all of the aspects are taken into consideration. The secretary becomes a master coordinator when conducting event planning assignments. Events can be successful when the boss and the secretary work together as a team. You need to be involved with the project throughout its life cycle.

9

How to Use a Microcassette for Dictation

It was inevitable that after the cassette player was invented it would be turned into a dictation machine. Before the dictation machine the boss either wrote drafts in longhand or dictated drafts to a secretary that could take shorthand. A secretary that could take shorthand was a highly paid executive level secretary, so the dictation machine provided a way for middle-management bosses to afford the upper management ability to dictate drafts. Then along came a small hand-held version of the dictation machine called a microcassette, which was inexpensive. This brought the ability of dictating drafts down to the level of an average salesperson. Unfortunately, the microcassette, and even the dictation machine for that matter, did not come with instructions on how to properly use it for dictating. This left the average-level secretary with the excruciating task of transcribing tapes full of poorly dictated drafts. The money saved in the ability to use the machine was lost in the time (hourly wage) it took to decipher the data. This problem still exists today.

The Dictation Process

Begin the dictation process by gathering all the information you will need to view as you are dictating. If you are dictating a response to a letter, obtain the original letter. If you are composing correspondence or preparing a report for a client, obtain the client file. Gather all the data you will need and put it in the order in which it is to be used. After you have completed your dictation project, the reference materials should remain in the order in which it was used and should be turned over to your secretary with the tape.

The next step for preparing the dictation is to think about what you are going to say before you dictate. Remember that when your secretary is transcribing the tape, she is typing at an even steady, pace. Stopping to go back and make corrections to a previously dictated sentence or paragraph makes the process of transcribing frustrating. If the dictation project is a long one, outline objectives with ideas for each paragraph before beginning. If you are answering a letter, pencil notes in the margins. Be completely prepared before you switch on that microcassette.

Begin the dictation by stating what you are dictating: "This is a sales report." Also, state the particulars of the end product, such as paper orientation, stationery, and format; for example, personal stationery or company letterhead, letter or legal size paper, portrait or landscape, interoffice memorandum, or formal block style. Also, state whether or not there is the need for envelopes to be printed.

Your secretary will return transcribed matter to you in draft form; therefore, if the output of the draft is to be different from the final product, indicate so at the beginning. For example, "Return draft in double-spacing."

If you are dictating several items that are to be placed on the same tape, be sure to do so in order of priority. It is not necessary to fill up a tape with dictation before giving it to your secretary. She will appreciate tapes with a small amount of items on them.

When speaking into the microcassette, pronounce your words clearly, precisely, and even with slower than normal speech. Keep in mind that your microcassette is not a telephone receiver and you are not having a conversation. Do not talk fast. Do not run your words together. Do not slur your words. Keep your mouth void of gum, cigarettes, writing utensils, food, cough drops, etc.

Spell all proper names; i.e., names of people, names of places, names of companies, etc. Spell words and numbers that can cause confusion. Keep in mind that you are making a mechanical recording and certain letters sound similar and can be misinterpreted when transcribing. For example, "f" and "v, t" and "d," "p" and "b," "sh" and "ch." It is in your best interest to spell words that are industry/technology specific, foreign words, and words that are not commonly used.

Indicate instructions to your secretary pertaining to the format and structure of the document; for example, new paragraph, bulleted indentions, table insertions, or placement of a graph. Begin instructions by getting your secretary's attention so that she won't type verbatim what you are telling her. This can be done by using her name: "Mary, indent the next five items with bullets."

57

When you are finished dictating the item, let your secretary know: "Mary, this is the end of the sales report." Immediately afterwards indicate distribution instructions. If distribution includes carbon copies (cc), be sure to supply properly spelled names and complete addresses; for example, fax letter, mail cc, hand deliver.

Summary of Dictation Rules

1. *Begin and end dictation* with announcements to your secretary; e.g., "This is the sales report," or "This is the end of the sales report."
2. *Pronounce your words clearly*, precisely, and even with slower than normal speech.
   - Do not talk fast
   - Do not run your words together
   - Do not slur your words
3. *Spell all proper nouns*; i.e., names of people, names of places, names of companies, etc.
4. *Make it clear* when you begin and end your sentences and paragraphs.
5. *Provide supporting documentation* with the cassette tape when presenting it to your secretary; i.e., file folder, complete names and addresses, phone numbers, etc.

10

The Forces Behind Producing a Document

Incorporating specific primary forces into document production will make the boss's working relationship with the secretary look like a well-performed song and dance routine. Coordination, communication, and choreography all take part in orchestrating a production, even a document production. You both need to understand the roles you play, and use the most effective tools available to achieve excellent results.

Presentation is everything! It's a paper matter act. How that paper looks represents you and your company. It is indicative of your style, level of professionalism, personality, and effort. It reveals a lot more about you than what you realize. We are inundated with paper matter in our society. If you want your piece of paper to be read, it has to look appealing and inviting. Not only that, you'd better make your selling points short and believable. Yes, selling! Whoever your audience may be, you are selling the subject matter for the purpose of being read. If your paper production actually gets read, you have succeeded. Too often printed matter gets a quick glance-over just prior to being filed or pitched. How many letters have you read all the way through? How many reports do you actually read all the way through? How many times have you had something filed for reference later after skimming its subject matter? Looking good on paper takes talent. It's an art.

As far as word processing programs are concerned, keep in mind that it is not the program, but the proficiency with which the program is used that makes the difference. The same can be said for all software programs used in an office environment, such as word processing, spreadsheets, databases, presentation programs, accounting, and calendar programs. It is the boss's responsibility to know enough about the software programs to understand their parameters, thereby having the ability to make assignments with realistically projected due dates. Depending on the desired finished product, the level of secretary makes a difference.

Professionalism and etiquette dictate specific styles in the realm of printed matter in the business world. Established styles in their proper format can be found in *The Gregg Reference Manual*. This book has been the best authority on the subject for almost fifty years. It is so thorough that it even explains how to properly fold a letter. Knowledge of such a simple thing as this could be assumed, but there are many people that have never been exposed to such basics. The boss needs to establish a standard style for the kinds of paper matter that is usually produced. There should be a separate style for business correspondence, internal manuscripts, and even notepaper

Chapter 10   *The Forces Behind Producing a Document*

size correspondence.

Usage of the English language—grammar, punctuation, spelling, and formulation of sentences—is the core of document production and is the basis of printed matter. Theoretically, a secretary should be an expert on the English language. Because of the complexity of the English language, very few people can make this claim. Also, the English language is changing. Those so-called well-established rules that were learned in school somehow keep changing. For example, the apostrophe is no longer used in plurals of capital letters or numbers, such as ATMs and 1850s. This puts printed matter in a crisis, as well as the secretary and her boss. How can you know what rules have been changed? Here again, *The Gregg Reference Manual* comes to the rescue. Any disputes about the proper use of the English language can be answered in this book.

A common error which unfortunately is being expounded by the word processing programs is the usage of the articles "a" and "an." The correct usage of "a" is before words that begin with a consonant sound, and "an" is used before words that begin with a vowel sound. The grammatical correcting part of word processing programs do not take into consideration that it is the sound of the beginning of the following word and not the actual letter of the word that determines the proper usage of the article; therefore, many people are erroneously using the articles "a" and "an" because of their dependency on the word processing programs to make this determination for them. This is only one of the grammatical check errors that word processing programs falsely display.

Another avenue to consider in keeping up-to-date on the English language is to pay for your secretary to attend some of the one-day seminars that are available throughout the country. You should be able to tap into your company's continuing education funds for this.

Proofreading is mandatory for document production, and it takes two sets of eyes to do it. That second pair of eyes is essential to produce top quality printed matter. Your secretary is the first pair of eyes. It is your responsibility as the boss to be the second pair of eyes. You must become an excellent proofreader. Learn to proficiently use the established set of proofreader's marks. Always use a red fine-point pen to make changes. Even in the simplest correspondences proofreading is necessary. When your secretary is working on a large document, she will become mesmerized by all the text and eventually become blind to needed corrections. This can also happen to you, that second pair of eyes. It is highly recommended to have yet another person proofing when it comes to documents with many pages. Never produce printed matter of any kind or size without proofreading.

Drafts are the working process through which printed matter becomes qualified for final output. They are for the purpose of editing. It is the quality control segment of document production. Always use a red fine-point pen to make changes. After your secretary has prepared the printed matter from your dictated tapes, pages of longhand, or her notes or compositions, she will return a draft to you. The draft should be in the paper style approved for the type of document that it is and printed on plain paper. The word "draft" should be printed with a colored pen on the top of the paper. There are pre-inked stamps made for this purpose. All drafts must be labeled as such to prevent confusion with redrafts. It also lets you know what stage of production the document is in. Numbering drafts in the sequence that they are produced is also recommended. After a draft has passed your inspection without any

Chapter 10   The Forces Behind Producing a Document

changes, you should write "ok to print" on the top of the paper and initial. It is your responsibility to approve the printing of the final document.

Signing documents seems to be what bosses do a lot of. Before you sign, review the document just as you would a personal contract. Your signature has power—be cautious in using it. Make a habit of always writing in the date beneath your signature or beneath your initials if you are initialing an item. A date is important. Keep in mind this proverb: *If it doesn't have a date, it holds no weight.* Documents and correspondences of all kinds must be dated.

Producing a document takes a shared effort from the boss and the secretary. You both take ownership of the printed matter produced in your name. Establishing procedures based on the guidelines in this chapter will help your document production go more smoothly. Turn to Chapter 11, Maintaining Standard Operating Procedures, for a scenario in producing correspondence.

63

11

Maintaining Standard Operating Procedures

Setting up and maintaining standard operating procedures for the functionality of the office and paper flow are as essential to your successful existence as a traffic light on a major intersection is to the safety of you and your automobile. It is necessary to follow certain regulations in order to achieve a professional image and to produce quality paper matter in a timely manner. Procedures should be set for the filing system, telephone, greeting visitors, processing mail and email, correspondence, and meetings. Setting up and maintaining these standards makes the boss appear to be in control. This is a key component to your image as a boss.

Chapter 11 Maintaining Standard Operating Procedures

The Filing System

Your data is only as good as your filing system. A filing system is for the purpose of storing documents in a convenient and consistent manner for easy retrieval. You and your secretary need to be able to find what you need, when you need it; therefore, it is important to establish a filing system that works for you.

Almost all files are arranged alphabetically. Just because you know the alphabet, does not mean that you know how to file. There are several nationally recognized filing standards. Your computer also has its own method of placing data in filing order. Your secretary should be well-acquainted with the rules that govern the proper methods of filing.

What part does the boss play in the filing system? First of all, you need to understand how it works. You should be able to retrieve documents when your secretary is not available. Secondly, it is your responsibility to direct the documents to be filed. This is best accomplished by using an alphabetical listing of your files. When a document crosses your desk that needs filing, you decide in whuch file it should be placed in by referring to your list, then label a sticky note with the file name and attach it to the document, or write the file name at the top of the paper in pencil. In this manner you will have a mental note of where it was filed. When your secretary files the document, she also will be making a mental note of it. Locating the document for retrieval will be easier because both of you took part in the filing process.

If your secretary has her own set of files, she needs to explain these to you so that you can access them, if necessary, when she is absent. Otherwise, it is best to go to her when you need contents from her files. The same should apply to personal files that you keep in your office. Having separate working files is necessary in a well-organized environment; nevertheless, it is important to communicate the purpose and contents of these files to each other. Never be the only one that knows your files.

A tickler file keeps track of items you wish to review or documents you will need at a future date. A commonly used method is monthly and numerically, representing the days of the month. It works like this: you received a report that you'll need to use to prepare a presentation for a conference on May 10. You want to review the report one month prior and also to be reminded of it. The document is filed in April. When April first arrives, your secretary pulls the items from April and places them in the numerical files that represent the days. She places the report in the file labeled "10." When the morning of the tenth arrives, she pulls the report and places it in your in-basket with a sticky note that reminds you that the document came from the tickler file and lists the reason it was originally placed there. Obviously, this system of filing only works if your secretary checks the tickler file daily. She'll be more apt to check it daily if you use it often.

Files can be a nightmare when they are large and cumbersome. For customer files there should be a specific order for the placement of documents within each file. For example, your customer files are four panel pressed cardboard with a two-hole punch bracket on the top of each panel. The first panel is for the original signed contract; the second is for all correspondence, with the most current on the top; the third is for productivity reports, with the most current on top; and the fourth is the payment record.

No one should remove a piece of information from a

Chapter 11   Maintaining Standard Operating Procedures

---

file. All files should remain intact. When information is needed from a file, the complete file should be used. When files are removed from the file cabinet, there should be a marker file to put in its place, or the keeper of these particular files should be notified. Files should never be torn apart or rearranged.

Filing is one of those duties most secretaries do not like to do. Unfortunately, to be "on top of it" and to maintain an organized atmosphere, it needs to be done on a regular basis. The best time to file is during slow periods when there's a break in the workflow. Keeping the filing up-to-date will keep the secretary informed. It is another aspect of the communication you share.

Telephone Protocols

Your secretary represents you and your company every time she answers the telephone or makes a call on your behalf. Her tone of voice and inflection of speech embed into the minds of callers a particular personality that is attached to your company name. She is the company and, by proxy, she becomes you. As the boss, you carry a certain amount of power that is transferred to your secretary every time she is called upon to represent you. Setting and maintaining telephone protocols for communications via the telephone is a vital part of your success.

A standard verbal greeting should be established for incoming calls. Greetings should be short and informative. Depending upon your preference, a "good morning" or "good afternoon" can preface it. If the boss's incoming line is direct and does not go through a switchboard, then it is appropriate to announce the company name. If it is not direct, then use the department name. Your name should

67

then be announced, for example, "John Smith's office." Depending upon your preference again, your secretary can announce her name after yours. Most callers like to know to whom they are speaking, so it is advisable to have your secretary announce her name. It can be a mouthful saying the whole string every time the phone is answered—time of day, company name, department name, boss's name, secretary's name. The best combination would be to keep it to three items. For example, if it was an incoming call that went through a switchboard first, then it might be answered as, "Sales Department, John Smith's office, Jane speaking." Greetings should be kept short, simple, and professional.

Is your secretary also a receptionist? Theoretically she is, but to what degree she is depends upon the level of secretary that you employ. Usually an administrative or executive level secretary answers only your personal extension and hers. Some administrative-level secretaries only answer a small departmental phone and theirs. In this case the boss usually has his line answered by his voice mail when absent. It is common for a small business or a large department to have a secretary or secretary/receptionist answer the main incoming lines.

Message-taking and retrieval is another one of those balancing acts that proves your communication skills. You need to set up a system that works for you. Almost all telephone systems have voice mail. It is acceptable and proper for your secretary to transfer a caller to your voice mail to leave a message. Sometimes a caller is adamant that a handwritten message be taken. You should designate a certain place for handwritten messages to be placed. It is a common practice to leave handwritten messages in the chair of the absent boss. In doing so the boss must physi-

Chapter 11 *Maintaining Standard Operating Procedures*

cally touch the message and therefore be aware of its contents. When handwritten messages are taken, the secretary should be sure to obtain specific pieces of information accurately, such as name of caller and caller's company, phone number, and purpose of call. She should make sure that she has spelled the caller's name correctly and repeat the phone number back to the caller. After the caller has hung up, she should write in the date and time of the call.

Screening the boss's calls is a typical secretarial duty. There are times when a boss instructs the secretary to hold the calls. The response that the secretary should make to the caller is that the boss is "not available." This is professionally acceptable. Naturally, there are certain calls that you will always take, like from the president or owner of the company, and from special customers. During your instructions to your secretary to hold your calls you must also reiterate the exceptions, even if they are standard operating procedures. Always be very thorough with your instructions to your secretary; leave nothing to be assumed. To assume means to make an "ass" out of "u" and "me."

Your secretary can do more than just answer the phone—that's why she's your secretary. She should be able to know your work well enough to provide answers to the incoming calls. In doing so she will relieve you from having to spend your time returning a call. To keep you informed as to the calls she answers on your behalf she should keep track of them, perhaps in her daily planner calendar, and review them with you at your weekly meeting with her.

For secretary/receptionist level secretaries, keep in mind that interruptions cause errors and answering phones causes interruptions. Herein lies the dilemma with this level of secretary. The error rate of a secretary increases with the amount of calls she must answer. When answering a main line is part of a secretary's duties, the amount of time it will take her to accomplish an assignment and the expected quality and error rate should be taken into account.

Greeting Visitors

People-contact of any kind is customer service. Keep in mind that the "customer" in customer service is not just literally the customer or client, it is "people" service. Customer service includes people-contact within an organization—company personnel, vendors, or customers/clients. Customer service begins within your own company. Contact with people can come in various forms, such as by telephone, in person, or through correspondence. Customer service skills must be used in these and all forms of people-contact.

People-contact takes diplomacy. When your secretary is associating with other company personnel, she is representing the boss. When the contact is directly on your behalf, the representation is obvious. What she may not realize is that she also indirectly represents you wherever she goes. She is an extension of the boss. She should keep in character with your expectations. If you have not specifically discussed this aspect of your working relationship with her, then you should seriously consider doing so. Internal company contact will probably be the majority of people-contact that she encounters.

Greeting external company visitors such as customers and vendors is normally the responsibility of a secretary, although some bosses prefer to do this on their own. When visitors arrive, your secretary should greet them in the

Chapter 11   Maintaining Standard Operating Procedures

lobby or reception area. Once again, diplomacy should govern her mannerisms. It is customary to conduct small talk in a conversational tone as the visitor is led to your office. If you have never personally met the visitor before, your secretary should make the introduction. After the meeting either you or your secretary should lead the visitor back to the lobby or reception area.

Greeting visitors is an excellent way for your secretary to get acquainted with your external company contacts. Your secretary needs to gain their confidence so that they will feel comfortable dealing with her on issues they have to take up with you. The more your secretary can do on your behalf, the more productive you will become. For this purpose it is important to build a trusting working relationship with your secretary.

Depending upon the level of secretary that you employ and the volume of people-contact associated with the position, your secretary may be required to have a professional appearance. A professional appearance usually equates to business dress attire. Do not expect your secretary to have a fabulous wardrobe when you pay her low wages. The average price of a professional-looking business suite is $150 - $200. Be sure that your expectations of your secretary are equivalent to the pay she receives. Too often secretaries are underpaid for the work they do.

Processing Mail

Mail is an information highway that is overloaded with a variety of printed matter designed to attract your attention. The onslaught of advertising in all of its colorful array is very alluring. We live in an age bursting with an over abundance of information that is published in magazines, newsletters, reports, books, and any means imaginable. Some of this information you may be interested in. Some bosses enjoy going through their "junk" mail, as it is called. Along with the piles of junk mail, there may even be a letter or two that is important and actually relevant to your work.

There is an art to processing mail and organization is the only way to achieve it. Think of organizing as the process of dividing in order to conquer. You and your secretary should have a system in place whereby you can quickly review and process your mail. Depending upon the level of secretary and your working relationship with her, you can delegate the authority of making the decision of which junk mail to pitch.

Dividing the mail is the first step toward organizing it. As it is opened, the secretary should review the contents and place them in categories. The categories that work best are as follows:

- Internal company correspondence
- External business-related correspondence
- Subscriptions, reports, and other material that has been requested
- Advertisements and other letter-sized junk mail
- Oversized junk mail including non-subscription magazines

There should be a color coded file folder designated for each category. For example, the red file folder is for internal company correspondence. Because you don't always have the time to review your mail on a daily basis like you should, there needs to be more than one folder for each color. For example, if there are three red folders, they should each have a label as follows: Internal #1, Internal #2, and Internal #3. Your secretary should keep track on

Chapter 11   Maintaining Standard Operating Procedures

her calendar or daily organizer which folder and its number you received on which date.

Some pieces of mail are marked "confidential" or "personal." Your secretary should not open these unless it is obvious that they are part of an advertiser's gimmick. The envelope or the sender's name and company should help her decide in which folder to place them.

A tracking system should be put in place to follow the life cycle of important mail. This is also an excellent way to track finalized documents that need your signature. Sometimes important pieces of mail get lost in the boss's office. For whatever reason, tracking specific mail and documents is worth the effort it takes to institute, for it is that ounce of prevention every boss should have. A simple handwritten log on notebook paper will work just fine. The category headings should consist of:

- Date received
- Received by whom–initials
- Sender's name
- Simple description of item
- Sent to whom
- Return date
- Returned by whom–initials

Once again, depending upon the level of secretary that you employ, and if it is a designated duty, she can jumpstart the return process by drafting a response to your incoming mail. If this is done, the draft should be paper-clipped to the back of the original correspondence and placed in the appropriate folder. Along these same lines, if the secretary recognizes correspondence from a client in which you would need to access the client file, she should pull the file and attach it to the colored mail folder to which it corresponds.

73

After your secretary has gone through all of the possible scenarios for processing the day's mail and has them divided into colored folders, she should then place them in your in-basket in your office. There may be items that she was unsure of how to place. These she will have to confer with you on. After you have emptied the contents of the mail folder, place it, empty, in your out-basket.

As you go through your mail you may want to forward certain pieces of mail or have your secretary make phone calls pertaining to it. For whatever miscellaneous instructions you may have, write them in simplicity on sticky notes, attach the notes to the front of the item, and place it in your out-basket. If you have drafted a response, attach it to the item and place in your out-basket.

You and your secretary should process mail on a daily basis. Having your secretary open and review your mail keeps her informed. The more informed she is the more committed she'll be.

Email Processing and Protocols

How personal is your email? Do you have the time to go through it? What volume of email do you receive? The answers to these questions will determine the feasibility of having your secretary go through your email, and the method you choose will determine the effectiveness of the method. Going through your email consists of reviewing and screening, which are entirely different functions.

Reviewing Email

In this method the secretary does not make any decisions pertaining to the data—she only presents them to you in a manner that you can act upon

Chapter 11   Maintaining Standard Operating Procedures

quickly. If they are printed out, acting upon them consists of writing instructions on them with a red pen and returning them to the secretary for her to follow through. If you acted upon some of the messages yourself, make a note on the messages as to what took place, then return to your secretary. If you answered the messages by sending an email, make sure to send a cc (carbon copy) or bcc (blind carbon copy) to your secretary. Remember that she read the initiating message, therefore, she will need to know its outcome. Email review should be a regular, daily duty.

Screening Email

If your secretary screens your email, a method of regurgitating the data is essential in order to provide you with the optimum time to address the issues presented. Screening consists of your secretary, usually an administrative level secretary, making the decisions on which messages are presented to you and in what manner they should be presented. She will automatically answer and follow through with messages in which she has the authority to do so, thus alleviating the mundane task from you. Presentation of the email message that the boss needs to personally advise and/or address should be presented to the boss on a regular basis. This is done by the secretary summarizing the message for a simple verbal presentation so that the boss can give quick instructions in response. At times the boss may need to view the original email message, so the secretary should always have a printed copy available. The weekly meeting is the prime time for the secretary to verbally review the email messages she addressed on your behalf.

Working with email software to set up shared access in order for your secretary to send email in your name is basic criteria for having your secretary review and/or screen your email from her computer. A procedure needs to be established for marking viewed messages if both the boss and the secretary sporadically view the boss's email. Making a directory in which to place the viewed messages is an option as long as the newly made directory is placed on the network so that both of you can access it. Email software programs automatically place these directories on the individual computer's hard drive of the person creating the directory. This can cause a dilemma, so be cautious when making these directories.

The best argument for having your secretary review your email is that it keeps her knowledgeable of what is going on in the company and keeps her informed of upcoming assignments. It keeps that communication flowing between you. Also, email is an excellent tool for documenting the workflow between you and your secretary, as well as other personnel.

There is another point of protocol that you should establish with your secretary that will keep you informed of her activities. When she corresponds with any internal company personnel that has a title equivalent to or greater than yours, she should always cc or bcc you. She should do the same with all external company contacts—customers, vendors, and the like. Of course, this only works if you take the time to regularly view your own email. It is also time-consuming but it keeps your job as her supervisor in perspective.

Correspondence Standards

The power of the written word stands forth as a sentinel against verbal attacks and rumors blowing in the wind. Correspondence is the business world's written word that is printed on company letterhead; its documentation power is solid and indisputable. Correspondence is an effective, professional means of communication that carries the stigma of importance—weightier than a phone call or an email. Email is a quick means of communication in which its composition has not gone through the process that makes it eloquent and properly effective. Choose wisely the method of correspondence you use in communication.

Letters and internal memorandums are the typical correspondence that you will produce on a regular basis. Letters are more formal than memorandums and can be used for external and internal company correspondence. Internal company memorandums are best used for short, cut-and-dried messages. On the opposite end of the spectrum are letters with their well-chosen words and long, flowery sentences. A memorandum is best used for announcements, directives, and impersonal, informative matter. Letters portray larger amounts of information with qualifying statements. Because of the informality of memorandums, they should only be used for internal company correspondence. Both letters and memorandums should be printed on company letterhead.

Establishing a standard format or style in which all of your correspondence should be produced is essential to portraying a professional image. For letters the standard styles to choose from are: block, modified block, and simplified. The basic elements of a letter include the date, addressee data, salutation, body or text, signature block, identification data, and distribution data. There is a variety of closing remarks found in the signature block that can be used. Some of these include: sincerely, best regards, cordially, and respectfully yours. The standard style you use, along with element variations such as in the closing remark, reflect your personality.

Memorandums are very simple in style, with the deviation being mainly in the header, for the elements consist only of a header, body or text, and identification data. For the "norm," memorandums do not have addressee data, a salutation, or a signature block, although they sometimes do have distribution data. Because of this, they are used for informal, internal company correspondence only. The elements of the header, which are listed in the order that they should appear, consist of: date, to, from, and subject or reference. The date should always be the first item in the header, just as it is the first item in a letter. Maintaining this standard of consistency with your correspondence production will make life easier for you and your secretary when filing or searching for a document.

The communication and material for correspondence should flow smoothly between you and your secretary. Chapter 10, The Forces Behind Producing a Document, brings into focus certain guidelines that should be followed in conjunction with the following scenario.

Scenario for Producing a Document

Step One: Presenting the Material

Initiating the process for producing correspondence usually falls upon the boss. The exception would be with administrative-level secretaries that have the responsibility to automatically compose

Chapter 11   Maintaining Standard Operating Procedures

correspondence drafts to incoming mail. Original material can consist of pages written by hand by the boss, dictated microcassette tapes, or notes your secretary has taken from you directly. Etiquette dictates that the boss should always provide supporting documentation with the original material. Supporting documentation is the information needed to do the job. With correspondence, this is the name and address of the person to whom it is being sent and the cc's as well. If you do not have this information, provide a phone number of someone to call that might have it. Your secretary is not a detective. She should not have to spend an hour hunting down an address. Other supporting documentation consists of anything to which the correspondence refers. For example, if the letter was to a customer, then the customer file should be provided. If the letter was an answer to a letter received, then attach the letter received. If you had written a letter and referenced a newspaper article, attach the article. Providing supporting documentation is one of the areas in which too many bosses lack, which brings to a halt the smoothness of the workflow.

Step Two: Preparation of the First Draft

The draft is a working copy of the correspondence; it is not the final product. You should never expect your secretary to produce a final product; e.g., a letter printed on letterhead from raw material. Why? Because to produce any correspondence with quality, even a two-sentence memo, you must go through the process of proofreading and editing. This takes two pairs of eyes—hers and yours. This

79

is your quality control!

Your secretary should prepare the correspondence according to your established styles for the type of correspondence it is. If you have established a standard for printing all drafts in double-space, then she should do so. The draft should be printed on plain white paper, then stamped at the top of the page with a "draft" stamp. For keeping track of the consecutive drafts, it is recommended that the draft also be numbered, "draft #1." She should then submit the draft to you with the original or raw material paperclipped behind it.

Step Three: Proofreading and Editing Drafts

It is the boss's responsibility to proofread and edit. Typically, proofreading is for correcting typographical, grammatical, and spelling errors. The established set of proofreader's marks should be used for this. Editing is for rearranging and restructuring sentences, paragraphs, and in general, the body of the text. The dictionary defines editing as "preparing for printing." This is exactly what you are doing. Finding errors and making changes is what this step is all about. Never, at any time, should you be accusatory toward your secretary for errors in drafts. Faultfinding is a negative behavior that breeds contempt and destroys a working relationship. When marking changes on the draft, you should always use a red fine-point pen. After all changes have been marked, return it to your secretary with the original or raw material paperclipped to it. You may want to personally go through the marked changes with your secretary so that she understands them as you intended. Interpretation is an individual matter and it is wise to dispel any possible confusion that may occur.

Step Four: Preparing the Next or Final Drafts

Your secretary should make all of the corrections you marked on the draft, then print it out again in draft form. This time she should stamp it "draft #2" and submit it to you with the first or next draft paperclipped behind it. For subsequent drafts you would use consecutive draft numbers.

Step Five: Proofreading the Next and Final Drafts

In the perfect scenario you wouldn't make any more editing changes, and the marked changes would have been done accurately. At this point you would write on the top of the draft with red fine-point pen, "okay to print," and initial. Return to your secretary with the previous draft attached. If you did mark changes, return to your secretary with the previous draft attached, and go back to step four. Do this until you receive a draft that you can send back to your secretary without any marked changes.

Step Six: Printing Correspondence

Your secretary should print the final version of the draft onto letterhead. She should also print any corresponding envelopes and all attachments referenced in the correspondence. She then should paperclip these together with the correspondence on top and submit it to you with a sticky note that reads, "ready for signature," or "please sign and return."

Step Seven: Review and Sign

This is your last chance to review this correspondence. Remember, you are responsible for the quality of the final product. For letters, sign your name in the signature block, and for memorandums you should initial beside your name in the header. Return to your secretary for distribution.

The document flow in this typical scenario for correspondence demonstrates the importance of a coordinated team effort between the boss and the secretary. Communicating respectfully with each other throughout the process is the tool that keeps it moving smoothly.

Procedures for Meetings

Meetings are for the exchange of information and ideas usually for the purpose of solving problems on a person-to-person level. Because of this personal aspect, there are a multitude of personalities involved that can cause a meeting to last a long time. Time is an expense to the company. Multiple salaries are being spent for the duration of the meeting; therefore, meetings should be short. As the boss, there are two procedures you need to follow to keep meetings productive, time-efficient, and cost-effective. Agendas and meeting minutes need to be developed, generated, and used.

Always have an agenda when conducting a meeting. Conducting a meeting on-the-fly is not conducive to producing lasting results. Your credibility is at stake when such components as an agenda are lacking in your management style. Agendas are the road map of a meeting that gives it purpose and direction. Without an agenda, meetings tend to take on a life of their own. It is a necessary control tactic.

What is the purpose of meeting minutes? To make a

Chapter 11 Maintaining Standard Operating Procedures

record of the proceedings for future reference of decisions made, items discussed, and tasks assigned. Meeting minutes are usually used for regularly held meetings. When minutes are needed for a singular meeting, the procedure is called meeting notes; nevertheless, they are the same thing and the same format can be used. For suggested formats of agendas and meeting minutes, refer to *The Gregg Reference Manual.*

When the assignment to set up a meeting is given to the secretary, it is the boss's responsibility to provide her with all of the pertinent information she needs to perform the task. The basics include the purpose of the meeting, the proposed agenda, who should attend, and a preferred place, date, and time. The crux of scheduling a meeting is coordinating the place, date, and time with all of the invited attendees. Scheduling meetings can be like pulling a lion's tooth.

For meetings that are not held on a regular basis, agendas should be prepared and sent to all of the attendees after the place, date, and time have been set. At the meeting copies of the agenda should again be distributed to the attendees as they arrive. If you are conducting the meeting you may want your secretary to prepare a copy of the agenda with your personal notes on it, or you may want to pencil in your own notes prior to the meeting.

For regularly held meetings a request for agenda items should be sent to all of the attendees, with a deadline, several days before the meeting. Immediately after the deadline the agenda should be prepared and distributed to the attendees before the meeting. At the meeting copies of the agenda should again be distributed to the attendees as they arrive.

This is the extent of an agenda. Its simplicity is overwhelming considering the powerful tool it can become. Agendas are also an excellent guide for the secretary to use when taking minutes. Meeting minutes are a lot more involved and will take up much more of your secretary's time.

If your secretary is required to take minutes or, in other words, notes of the proceedings, she should keep in mind that she is not writing a book and should steer away from the "he said," and "she said," dogma. She should jot down one-liners that pertain to a decision made, an item discussed, or an assignment given. Use the following steps to prepare the meeting minutes.

Preparing Meeting Minutes

Step One

In preparing the first draft of the minutes, your secretary should follow the agenda items in the order in which they were listed. This will eliminate confusion. This is best done by first listing the agenda items as they appear on the agenda, then making a paragraph out of the notes taken. To cut out the garble, sentences should be statements packed with evidence.

Step Two

After the first draft has been prepared, it should be submitted to you. It is your responsibility to verify its contents and to proofread and edit it. Changes should be made with a red fine-point pen. Never add material that was not presented at the meeting.

Step Three

Return the first draft to your secretary with

Chapter 11   Maintaining Standard Operating Procedures

marked changes. She will then make the changes and print a final draft.

Step Four

Your secretary should submit the final draft to you with the first draft paperclipped behind it. This time around, it is your responsibility to verify that the changes have been made. If the final draft was satisfactory, you should write with red pen at the top of the page, "okay to print," and initial. If it was not satisfactory, you should go through as many rounds of drafts as necessary to achieve a draft free of changes.

Step Five

The approved final meeting minutes are then printed and submitted to you for initialing beside your name, which should be printed at the top of the page as the person conducting the meeting, then return to her for distribution.

Step Six

Your secretary should then make copies of the initialed meeting minutes and distribute to all of the attendees.

Step Seven

The secretary should file the original, initialed meeting minutes in a file specifically prepared for this purpose.

At the next meeting a copy of the meeting minutes are again distributed to the attendees. The first agenda item at the current meeting should be to approve the minutes of the previous meeting. Then the cycle begins all over again.

12

The Boss's Working Relationship With Other Office Personnel

Too often bosses get so used to giving commands that they don't think through before they speak. They don't pay attention to whom they are giving what command. They put every one of a clerical status in the same category and don't differentiate between titles and responsibilities. This insensitivity causes hardships on those who have a working relationship with a boss of this nature.

It is your responsibility to understand the duties of each employee with which you associate and what the perimeters of your working relationship should be with them. You must also distinguish the duties of your secretary from the duties of the other secretaries, and learn what is socially appropriate to ask of other office personnel without overstepping the realm of their duties and the boundary of office politics. This is a potentially explosive area that takes effort on your part to learn and perceptiveness to handle on a daily basis. The boss that does not fully understand and appreciate each employee's respective duties in relation to the boss and the secretary will inevitably cause discord among the ranks.

The receptionist is a central figure in any office and has the mega-responsibility of representing the company, not you. It is your secretary's responsibility to represent you. Never at any time should you give the receptionist any assignment that falls within your secretary's job description. If the receptionist is also a word processor and you would like to utilize her availability, give the assignment to your secretary to delegate to her. The secretary then becomes the contact person for the assignment. This keeps the secretary informed of all of your dealings, as she should be, and keeps that harmonious communication flowing between the two of you. If you work for a small company of 50 or less employees or in a department large enough to have its own receptionist, either you or your secretary should keep the receptionist informed of visitors and planned absences. If the receptionist is the one that receives overnight deliveries, courier deliveries, or deliveries in general, it is a common courtesy to inform her of any expected deliveries. This should be the duty of your secretary. Besides a friendly hello and personal conversations, there isn't much else to your working relationship with the receptionist.

In dealing with other secretaries, there is only one thing you must remember—they are not your secretaries! Just because they have a secretarial title does not mean that you can give them assignments because you have a boss title. You should never give another secretary an assignment. Never ask your secretary to delegate an assignment to another secretary unless that kind of working relationship has been developed with the other secretary, and it is acceptable to do so in the office in which you work. In general, secretaries should not receive assignments from other secretaries. Keeping your secretary informed is the basis of communicating with her. When you ask another secretary to do a task for you, it takes your secretary out of the loop. It breaks the communication cycle which destroys the kind of working relationship you should be building with her.

If you are a boss that has both a secretary and an administrative assistant, you must be on your guard at all times. If you are a boss working in a small business or department in which there are several secretarial or clerical type positions that are not clearly defined, you must be on your guard also. Beware of giving the same assignment, inadvertently, to two different people. Discussing something that needs to be done can be viewed by a responsible secretary as an assignment. Repeatedly talking about the item that needs to be done can cause another employee to act upon the information in the same manner. When the duplicate assignment is discovered, it causes conflict and hurt feelings. Remember that because you are a boss, what you say is taken seriously; therefore, what you say should be decisive and thoughtfully reflective of your own title and position.

The accounting and financial office personnel usually have responsibilities that are not in direct competition with your secretary. Depending upon the level of secretary that you employ, and the types and amounts of accounting and financial responsibilities she has, the boss should be able to appropriately give assignments to these other departments. It is common for an administrative-level secretary to have a lower-level amount of accounting and financial responsi-

Chapter 12 The Boss's Working Relationship With Other Office Personnel

bilities. She usually works directly with these departments on a daily basis. Communication is still the key here. During your weekly meetings inform your secretary of your dealings with these departments, especially if they will reflect upon her future workflow.

Your secretary and the other office personnel have a society all their own. Don't get involved with the politics in the office amongst the clerical staff. If per chance someone tries to drag you in, find a way to kindly bow out. Learn to distinguish between office politics and conflicts that need a mediator to help resolve them. Don't get involved in the thermostat wars—every office has them. Be aware of the office politics going on around you—it may influence your future decisions. If you have a good rapport with your secretary, she should be the one that shares this information with you. Being aware and being involved are two separate things—keep them separate.

13

Finding the Right Secretary

Secretarial Pay Scale

The secretary is a human being with limits. The "girl-friday" of yesteryear was a "do-all," self-sacrificing woman with a thankless wage and a demanding boss. She no longer exists. The newest version of this superhuman model is the "can-do" secretary that rolls up her sleeves and digs in. She's dedicated and is willing to make sacrifices, including working late, provided she is compensated with a handsome salary and the freedom of a flexible schedule for time off. The cliche, "you get what you pay for" rings true with the level of secretary you hire.

There are two main factors to consider when looking for the right secretary. The first is the level of secretary that is needed. The levels are divided into five of the most commonly used titles in the United States. For administrative-level titles they are administrative assistant, executive secretary, and administrative secretary. The average- and entry-level secretary titles are secretary and secretary/receptionist. See Chapter 3, The Different Levels of Secretaries, for more details on the title breakdown. The second factor is the amount of salary budgeted for the secretarial position.

The secretary's title and salary are directly related to her work experience and education. As can be expected, a college degree of any kind demands a higher salary. The highest salary is budgeted to the secretary that has attained the CPS (Certified Professional Secretary) rating. Work experience in the secretarial profession is equivalent to a college degree. The college degree does not prove that she can be a secretary unless her transcript shows secretarial courses; nevertheless, the secretarial profession is commonly learned through hands-on experience. The more work experience in the field, the greater the skill level, attributes, and professionalism the secretary will have obtained. Here again, the more experience in the field, the greater the salary. For administrative-level secretaries it is the combination of college, degreed or not, and work experience that will demand the higher salaries. Use the work experience and education tables in determining the level of secretary to hire and in evaluating the secretarial candidate.

Work Experience
0 – 2 years
2 – 5 years
5 – 10 years
10 – 15 years
15 – 20 years
20+ years

Education
High school
Some college
AA degree
BA degree
MA degree
CPS rating

The number of skills and the level of work in which they are expected to be used in the secretarial position respectively increase the salary that should be paid. Liken this to using a shopping cart in a store. As you go down the aisle and select items to place in your cart, the more items placed in the cart, the higher the tally will be at the checkout stand. Some skills are simply a matter of being able to do, while others are dependent upon the level in which they can be executed.

Skills are divided into four categories: general, developed, typing, and software. All secretaries are expected to have the general skills. The developed skills are usually learned through experience. The ability the secretary has to perform these skills needs to be evaluated with the proficiency and style in which they are executed in determining their salary value. Manual dictation demands the highest salary. Typing speed has always been a determining factor in the pay scale. Software skills and the level of expertise in which they are used also impacts the salary level.

Use the skills tables to determine the necessary skills for your secretarial position, then determine the reality of the budgeted salary for the position. You may have to cut back on the skills requirements in order to keep it in line with the budgeted salary range.

General Skills	
Telephone etiquette	
Phone systems	
Voice mail systems	
Spelling / grammar	
Copy machine	
Facsimile machine	
Ten key or calculator	

Developed Skills	
number of years expereince	
Scheduling	
Event planning	
Meeting minutes	
Writing / composition	
Editing / proofreading	
Math / numbers	
Accounting/bookkeeping	
Transcription	
Manual dictation	

Typing Speed	
wpm = words per minute	
up to 25 wpm	
26 – 35 wpm	
36 – 45 wpm	
46 – 55 wpm	
56 – 65 wpm	
65+ wpm	

Software Skills	1	2	3
Word processor			
Spreadsheet			
Database			
Financial / accounting			
Electronic mail			
Calendar			
Presentation			
Web browser			
Wed page maintenance			
Web page design			
Desktop publishing			

1 = beginning
2 = average
3 = advanced

The attributes are a pivotal point in determining the level of secretary to hire. Attributes are an inherent quality or personal characteristic that enhance the manner in which the responsibilities to the secretarial title are carried out. Certain attributes have high price tags, while the majority can be accumulated and tallied as was described in the skills shopping cart scenario.

An administrative-level secretary should have the higher-priced attributes, which are: organization, communication, self-starter, detail-oriented, confidentiality, professionalism, and leadership. While the combination of these higher-priced attributes determines the highest salary, they can be selected individually along with other attributes not listed on this list in an accumulation of attributes that does not carry as high of a salary. It is the use of each of these higher attributes that add up. For example, your secretarial position needs someone that is detail-oriented, which raises the salary in greater proportions than attributes individually selected from those that are not listed as part of the higher attributes list.

Use the attributes tables in determining the attributes preferred for the secretarial title for which you are recruiting. Once again, the proficiency in which these attributes are executed is just as important a determining factor for the salary offered as the reality of the combination of attributes selected. Be reasonable in your expectations.

Higher Attributes	
Organizational	
Communication	
Self-starter	
Detail-oriented	
Confidentiality	
Professionalism	
Leadership	

Chapter 13 Finding the Right Secretary

Attributes	
Team player	Take-charge
Interpersonal	Goal-oriented
People motivator	Good judgment
People-oriented	Analytical
Office etiquette	Bilingual
Energetic	Creative
Enthusiasm	Flexibility
Positive outlook	Punctuality
Decision maker	Stability
Problem solver	Maturity
Versatility	Quick study

In determining the qualities for a secretarial position the four categories—education, work experience, skills, and attributes—need to be carefully reviewed. Items selected from each of them should be in line with the budgeted salary range and the actual needs of the position. During the search process candidates should be interviewed in a manner that will provide a summary of their qualities to compare with those selected from the four categories. The candidate summary table is designed to help with this.

Candidate Summary	
Experience	
Education	
Attributes	
Typing speed	
General skills	
Developed skills	
Software skills	

95

Word of caution: when conducting interviews, make sure that the questions you ask are legal. By law, it is illegal to ask any questions pertaining to religion, marital status, number of children, race, and personal statistics such as age, weight, height, etc. The reasoning is that you cannot use any of this kind of criteria in your evaluation process for hiring employees. It is in your best interest to learn about these laws. Also, learn the labor laws that govern the secretarial position; there are two levels—federal and state. The more knowledgeable you become on employment and labor laws, the better qualified you'll be to address issues pertaining to them.

Matching Personalities

Finding the right secretary takes more than formulating a list of qualifications that include work experience, education, skills, and attributes. It's a personality match. No matter how qualified the secretarial candidate may be, the ultimate hiring decision is always based on personality. It has been proven time and time again that a lesser-qualified candidate will get the job because her personality was favorable to the personality of the boss. If this one fact were recognized more, human resources departments and employment agencies would find greater success in the retention rate of new hires.

During the interviewing phase of the job search the social aspect of the personality match takes place without the boss even knowing it. It begins with the first impression, which is based on the visible character traits that appear to be pleasing. Throughout the interview the boss will subconsciously send out character signals for reception on the other end. A favorable response is the aspect of the personality upon which the boss bases the hiring decision.

Chapter 13 Finding the Right Secretary

This is most unfortunate, for it is the other aspects of the personality that are the true basis for compatibility.

The other aspects of the personality that had not been determined pertain to the work habits, accustomed working conditions, and personal preferences that can affect a working relationship. Evaluating only the interviewee's is not sufficient. The boss also needs to be evaluated. It is the comparison of the two that is the basis for compatibility.

What is true compatibility? Here again is an area in which there is much deception. Mathematics helps us find a clue to the answer in the equation; two positives equal a negative. The interpretation being that if the boss and the secretary have all the same characteristics, then they are not truly compatible for there is nothing to balance out the faulty characteristics. The true balanced compatibility of characteristics is a soft opposite. Some of the characteristics should be the same, but there should be enough slightly opposing characteristics that complement each other and balance out the weak ones. Complete opposites which go to the other end of the scale are negative and not compatible.

The simple questions in the following quiz can be used in determining the working characteristics of the boss and the secretary. Compare the answers and evaluate whether the likenesses or differences are complementary to each other in your working environment.

The boss-secretary working characteristics compatibility quiz

1. Most productive time of day   boss   secretary
- Early morning ☐ ☐
- Midmorning ☐ ☐
- Early afternoon ☐ ☐
- Late afternoon ☐ ☐
- Evening ☐ ☐

2. Preferred begin work time   boss   secretary
- Before 7:00 a.m. ☐ ☐
- 7:00 – 7:30 a.m. ☐ ☐
- 7:30 – 8:00 a.m. ☐ ☐
- 8:00 – 8:30 a.m. ☐ ☐
- 8:30 – 9:00 a.m. ☐ ☐
- 9:00 – 9:30 a.m. ☐ ☐
- 9:30 – 10:00 a.m. ☐ ☐
- Later then 10:00 a.m. ☐ ☐

3. Working overtime   boss   secretary
- Strongly dislike ☐ ☐
- Will if necessary ☐ ☐
- Sometimes ☐ ☐
- Agreeable anytime ☐ ☐
- Almost daily ☐ ☐

4. Leaving work at end of day   boss   secretary
- Prefer to leave early ☐ ☐
- Must leave on time ☐ ☐
- Usually leave on time ☐ ☐
- Leave late occasionally ☐ ☐
- Leave late almost daily ☐ ☐

5. Taking breaks   boss   secretary
- Always ☐ ☐
- Usually ☐ ☐
- Sometimes ☐ ☐
- Rarely ☐ ☐
- Never ☐ ☐

6. Listening to music at desk   boss   secretary
- Prefer on all day ☐ ☐
- Occasionally during day ☐ ☐
- Will tolerate music ☐ ☐
- Does not like music on ☐ ☐

7. Food / beverages at desk   boss   secretary
- Beverage always at desk ☐ ☐
- Snacks throughout the day ☐ ☐
- Always eats lunch at desk ☐ ☐
- Usually eats lunch at desk ☐ ☐
- Sometimes eats lunch at desk ☐ ☐
- Never eats lunch at desk ☐ ☐
- Don't like food at desk ☐ ☐
- Don't like beverage at desk ☐ ☐

There are other idiosyncrasies that should be evaluated in determining the possible compatibility of the working relationship between the boss and the secretary. They could include such questions as:

- ☐ Is accuracy more important than meeting a deadline?
- ☐ Do unfinished assignments cause pressure?
- ☐ Do deadlines become a last minute crisis?

These are thought-provoking questions that should be answered in an essay format with an example to back up the answer. These should then be discussed.

Matching the personalities of the boss and the secretary is an integral factor in hiring the right secretary, and it plays an important role in retaining her. It is also a key component to developing a harmonious working relationship.

The Hiring Edge

What does the boss have to offer the prospective new-hire secretary that makes the secretarial position better than the others? Any employer can offer a good salary so outside the realm of the duties performed, what makes your secretarial position so special? The answer is perks. Perks are those value-added commodities that provide a means for working conditions to be more amicable. Although perks are usually an expense to the employer, they make a world of difference in the office.

The most common perk is free coffee. In line with that is free tea, hot chocolate, and sometimes sodas. When perks are free, they are the most effective. Friday-morning donuts are a favorite.

Besides regular daily and weekly perks, there are those holiday perks that pull a lot of weight with employees. For instance, on Secretary's Day, a bouquet of flowers; for Thanksgiving, a gift certificate for a turkey at a local grocery store; and for Christmas, that bonus check.

Not all perks are free. There are the low-cost perks like a soda machine with soda for only 25¢, or the hot beverage machine with coffee and hot chocolate for 10¢. Even though consumable goods make excellent perks, there are others that can be more persuasive in the new-hire search.

Working conditions can be the most powerful and persuasive perks you can use. Is the computer at the secretary's desk a newer model with all the bells and whistles? Tell her so. For the amount of time a secretary uses a computer and the quality of documents she's expected to produce, the computer can be just the right perk.

Is there a window at the secretary's desk? Eight hours a day surrounded by walls and cubical dividers that goes on year after year is depressing. A window is a coveted commodity.

The daily work schedule can be turned into the most valuable perk of all. An early riser may prefer to work 7:30 a.m. to 4:00 p.m., with a half-hour for lunch. Getting off at 4:00 p.m. in the afternoon may be a very important factor to a secretary with school-aged children. Perhaps a work schedule of 8:30 a.m. to 5:30 p.m., with an hour for lunch, is preferred in order to avoid the heavier traffic in traveling to and from work. A work schedule that allows every other Friday off is a secretary's dream. This works out well with a bi-weekly payroll. Those that have had the privilege of such a schedule use that free-day for doctor's appointments and other personal business transactions that can only be done during regular working hours. This "free-day" costs the employer nothing and would make a tremendous difference in the workforce.

Let the prospective new-hire secretary know about these perks. They are the most overlooked attribute the boss has to offer. Perks are also the most underdeveloped means for improving a secretarial position. They do make a difference.

14

How to Work With a New Secretary

The boss's working relationship with the secretary is rooted in the first few weeks on the job. The style in which you work together is developed during this crucial time period. Work habits are established and routines are formulated. It is a sensitive time. Reproving should be withheld until a bank of praise has been put in place.

Even though you have hired a secretary with excellent qualifications, she will not know the particulars of your secretarial position. You will need to train her in the standards that you have established. She will need to be taught how you prefer your telephone answered, your method of filing and processing mail, your preferred styles for correspondence, how you want your name and title typed, and other such procedures that you have set.

Basic lists that a secretary needs in order to do her job

Chapter 14   How to Work With a New Secretary

include: a company-wide telephone list, a department telephone list, a list of preferred vendors, a list of internal company contacts with whom the boss regularly works, a list of nearby restaurants and also eating establishments that deliver, a list of customers for whom the boss is responsible, and a list of email addresses for all employees and customers. Providing your new secretary with such lists lets her know that you care and are conscious of the work she does. She will be working hard to do a good job. She has a tremendous amount to learn, especially the names of all her coworkers and the names of those she contacts by phone.

All computers are different. Take the time to show her how to power up and shut down her computer. If a password is needed to get onto the network, you should take the time to obtain one for her before her first day at work. The same should be done with long distance telephone passcodes. Any keys to the office, department, or building that she will need should also be prepared in advance.

The boss needs to expect to spend an extended amount of quality time with the new secretary, instructing her in all aspects of the secretarial position. Even the simplest functions should be reviewed with her; leave no stone unturned. If you are thorough in this training phase it will pay off later. Never assume what she knows. The quality time you spend with her and the caring manner in which you train her will build the trusting working relationship that is vital to your success.

The first week on the job can be touch-and-go as you are getting to know each other and simultaneously learning how to work together. The following is a guideline for the first week.

Day One

Introductions are in order. Introduce your new secretary to everyone within the company that she may have dealings with—don't forget to introduce her to the receptionist. Show her where the lunchroom and other eating facilities and vending machines are located. She'll need to know where to find the mailroom, restroom, and copy machine. If there are specific regulations for parking, employee entrances, employee badges, and the like, explain these to her on the first day. Have her spend time reviewing her job description and list of duties, then meet with her and go over them thoroughly. This is the time for you to discuss your expectations of her on all issues, then let her spend time getting familiar with her work area, computer, and telephone. Provide her with instructions for setting up the voice mail announcement on her extension. During this first week avoid a heavy document production workload. Let her get acquainted with the computer and the directories in which your work is stored. She should review these directories to familiarize herself with your styles and the type of work you produce.

It is acceptable for you to take your new secretary to lunch, along with another secretary of the same level or someone else in the office with whom she will be working on this first day. This is a good time to share personal information about each other such as your families, hobbies, etc. In the afternoon have her learn your calendar system, and review the filing system. This is a good time to have her do some filing. Filing is an excellent way to find out what you and the job are all about. End the day by meeting with her and going over the things that she has learned. Be sure to ask her if she has any questions.

Day Two

Meet with your new secretary first thing in the morning. Ask her how she is and spend some time conversing on non work-related subjects before you turn to work-related issues. Thoroughly go over your telephone protocols so that she can begin answering your line, then introduce her to your schedule. This will be the first time she has seen it. Go over your calendar and the projects you are working on. Give her some assignments and then be available for questions. Remember that you are easing her into your workload. Do not throw her in lock, stock, and barrel. You don't want to overwhelm her just yet. Be sure to compliment her on her accomplishments. Check with her as often as you can to see if she has any questions. At the end of the day meet briefly with her. Ask her how her day went, and ask again if she has any questions.

Days Three and Four

Meet with your secretary first thing in the morning to give her direction in her workflow. Always begin the meeting conversing on non work-related subjects. Be available as much as you can be during the day to answer questions. Remember that during her learning curve she is not up to speed. As you observe her abilities to handle the assignments, introduce her to more aspects of her job. Be sure to build her confidence by commending her for a job well-done. Again, meet with her for a short time at the end of the day to see how her day went, and ask if she has any questions.

Day Five

Your new secretary should be getting the hang of things. She should be feeling like she is being productive and doing a good job. She should be comfortable with the phones, your calendar, and document production. Meet with her extensively to review all that she has learned this week. Remember to begin the meeting by spending some time conversing on non work-related subjects. Review again her job description and list of duties. Discuss your calendar and workflow and how she fits in. Discuss your observations of her abilities and learning curve. Give her a time frame for introducing the duties she has not yet learned and set goals that will be reviewed at her first performance review. Set up a regular day and time for your weekly meetings with her. Compliment her for the fine job she is doing. At the end of the day let her know you've enjoyed working with her during the week, you hope she has a nice weekend, and you look forward to working with her next week.

It takes about a year for the new secretary to truly become efficient in her position. Businesses and industries of all kinds have an annual life cycle in which certain events, processes, and procedures take place. The holidays and seasons of the year also affect this life cycle. Efficiency comes through experiencing all the events that take place during a full twelve months in the same position. The boss's working relationship with the new secretary is gradually developed through the year.

15

Ergonomics and the Secretary's Health

It's just another responsibility the boss has: the far reaching effects of the hazards in the workplace on the secretary's health. As though the wide spectrum of the working relationship wasn't enough, now you have to add the secretary's health. Who would have thought that the invention of the computer would end up causing so much havoc in the workplace. This havoc has a name and it's called ergonomics, which somehow boils down to meaning health issues stemming from the work environment.

It all began with the computer. To be more specific, with the monitor, which is called a video display terminal. Radiation is the culprit. The monitor emits a radiation in the form of a magnetic field with electromagnetic waves. What causes the monitor to be hazardous? Two factors are involved in the answer. First and foremost is the distance between the secretary and the monitor during its use. The second is the amount of time spent using the monitor at a close range.

What can be done to protect the secretary? To begin with, distance makes a difference. Magnetic radiation levels decrease in proportion to the distance from the source. The recommendation is to keep a distance of 24-36 inches from the front and three feet from the back and sides of the monitor. Another avenue of protection to pursue is a grounded filter. This is a screen that is placed over the monitor screen that is grounded. Do not confuse this with the nonglare filters that are not grounded. It is the grounding that helps to reduce the radiation. No matter what the manufacturer claims, these filters can only block the electromagnetic waves and not the magnetic field. If radiation is a problem for the secretary, then have her turn off the monitor when it is not in use.

It may not be possible to reduce the many hours your secretary spends in front of the computer but breaking up that time can give her some relief. Taking a 15-minute break away from the computer is recommended. Besides the recommendation, it's the law. Federal labor laws require two 10 to 15 minute breaks and one half-hour minimum lunch break in an eight-hour work day. State labor laws may vary. The 10 to 15 minute break should be taken away from the computer and work area, otherwise the break won't be effective in reducing the effects of radiation from the monitor.

What health problems can the computer cause? The eyes seem to be affected the most. A deterioration of vision due to computer use is the most common and surprisingly accepted health hazard. More specifically, shortsightedness is the most prevalent. Eyestrain can cause blurred vision, double vision, and red eyes, and let's not forget those headaches. Computers can cause headaches.

The computer and the secretary's workstation are the central points for many other health-related issues. The types of injuries that are a result of using an office workstation are called musculoskeletal disorders (MSDs). They affect the joints, muscles, spine, nerves, tendons, and cartilage. Such injuries are carpal tunnel syndrome, tendinitis, muscle spasms, herniated disks, lower back pain, and sciatica. These injuries are a result of poor posture and positioning, repetitive movements, body strain, and lifting while executing the work, usually at the workstation.

The items in the work area that the boss needs to pay attention to are the chair, keyboard, position of computer, and lighting. What are the concerns of these items, and how can stress from these items be reduced? The answers are as follows.

Chair

The right chair encourages good posture and relieves stress on the lower back, neck, and muscles. There are a large variety of ergonomic chairs on the market. Look for one with a lumbar support in the back rest. Adjusting the chair to fit the secretary is just as important as the right chair. When she is siting in the chair, her feet should be flat on the floor or a foot rest, and there should be no pressure against the upper leg near the seat edge. The back rest should be at an angle equivalent to the inward curve of the spine in the lower back, then the pressure in the lumbar support should be adjusted to suit the secretary's needs.

Keyboard

It is the repetitious downward wrist movement that takes place when using the keyboard that can cause carpal tunnel syndrome. Both the keyboard and the position of the keyboard while typing can be addressed. Again, there are ergonomic keyboards. They are designed with the keys of the keyboard split, with half slanted to the right and half slanted to the left and the backside raised slightly vertically. This keyboard is designed to encourage the proper position of the secretary while in use. This position consists of keeping the wrists straight with a slight incline and the arms relaxed with the upper arm vertical and the elbows bent to a 90° angle. The forearms should not be outstretched, and the mouse should be within range, also without stretching.

Position of Computer

Once again we go back to the central figure—the computer. To help prevent shoulder, head, neck, and eye strain, the monitor should be placed at a 10°-15° angle below eye level. It is also recommended that a copyholder be used that will hold materials vertically.

Lighting

The glare from the computer and fluorescent lights are the harmful elements. Improper lighting not only causes eye strain but also headaches. There are several recommendations. Let's address the monitor first by turning up the brightness above that of the light in the room, then the monitor should be positioned so that it is at an angle perpendicular to the windows. The window should not be directly in front or behind the monitor. Fluorescent lighting may be beyond your control; nevertheless, the ambient light level should be between 30-50 foot candles.

Providing a health conscious workstation for your secretary is one of those things you do because you care. Providing the secretary with the tools needed to do the job is your responsibility. Showing you care is one of the tools you use to build a harmonious working relationship. Show your secretary how much you care.

16

Supervising the Secretary

Every team needs a leader, and the boss is the leader of the boss-secretary team. A leader shows the way by example and through influence via kind persuasion. Influencing the behavior of the secretary is the objective. A highly productive secretary can be the result of positive behavior.

What behavior does the boss want from the secretary? How about loyalty. How can the boss get the secretary to be loyal? By showing her trust. By showing a concern for her well-being. By showing common courtesy and respect. Loyalty can go a long way in a working relationship. A loyal secretary quickly becomes a crusader on your behalf anytime the need arises. She'll defend your name in the battle zone of the office. She'll do whatever it takes to get the job done. Loyalty is a behavioral trait that every boss should strive to obtain. The tools with which to influence

Chapter 16   Supervising the Secretary

behavior are discussed in Chapter 4, The Boss's Working Relationship With the Secretary.

Leading the team by example accrues respect. Respect is high admiration. What boss wouldn't want admiration from the secretary? Setting an example also means doing what you expect others to do. For example, it just doesn't cut it when the boss expects the secretary to be to work at 8:00 a.m. sharp, and the boss moseys in around 9:30 a.m. or so every day. Without the example the expectation becomes noneffective, and respect is lost.

Besides being the leader of the team, the boss also has to be the secretary's supervisor. To supervise is to oversee the execution of the work. In order for the boss to supervise the secretary's work, two factors need to be determined. The first factor is a firm description of duties and responsibilities. If this has not been set in place, the supervisor has no leverage, and the supervising loses its credibility.

The second factor is the skill level of the secretary. This should have been a requirement for the position. An administrative-level secretary is highly skilled so the execution of the work does not need overseeing, only periodic reviewing. An entry-level secretary/receptionist has basic skills; therefore, the execution of the work will need overseeing. Overseeing the secretary's work and micromanaging are two completely different things. Micromanaging is what supervisors do when they personally get involved in all of the details of the work to the point of suffocation. The supervisor should train the secretary, trust her to use her own judgment, and then oversee and/or review only when necessary.

An important part of supervising is being a teacher. Your teaching skills are used extensively when you are training a new secretary, and they are periodically used

113

throughout the working relationship no matter how long you've worked together. The new secretary's skill level will determine how quickly she learns the standard operating procedures you have established. A training schedule should be followed for the entry-level secretary/receptionist which should move forward at a pace that her skill level allows. The attributes the boss should exercise while executing the responsibility of teacher is that of patience and understanding.

No one is born a boss. Leading and supervising skills have to be developed. These skills are constantly challenged through the personality traits and behavior issues that surround the boss, the secretary, and their combined working relationship. How can the boss know when the leading and supervising methods need changing or improving? By listening for feedback. Listening involves reading the secretary and reading the situations that take place throughout the day. Feedback can also be received by directly asking the secretary what you want to know. She should be your sounding board. These are tools the boss can use to glean an insight into the direction to go in order to guide the working relationship.

Being a boss is challenging. Leading and supervising is something that has to be practiced every single day. Be the kind of boss your secretary can look up to.

17

The Performance Review

The best tool there is for encouraging growth in the working environment is through performance reviews. The word appraisal is another term used in lieu of review. This brings into focus another aspect of this tool—to estimate the secretary's value. The secretary is of great value to the boss. Estimating the value of the secretary for the purpose of encouraging growth on the basis of the manner in which the work was executed is what a performance review is all about.

The performance review is not the time to reprove events of the past. The problems of the past should have been addressed and resolved in the past and not during the review. Criticism should have no part in the review. See Chapter 4, The Boss's Working Relationship With the Secretary. If improvement is needed, it should be presented in a constructive, kind, and helpful manner.

The review can have negative connotations if an attitude of judgment is used. Judging portrays a critical action, as in condemning. It puts the boss high above the secretary, like sitting in judgment. The boss and the secretary are supposed to be a team. Even though the boss is the lead, the attitude of "I'm better than she" is not conducive to the working relationship at any time, including during the review process. Rather, an attitude of "let's look at this together" is the angle in which it should be approached.

The review is based on the work executed by the secretary; therefore, a list of her duties and responsibilities are necessary. This should be included in her job description. The first step in the performance review begins with the boss writing an evaluation. Remember that this is done by estimating the value of each duty for the purpose of encouraging growth. There are two general written formats that can be used.

The first performance review format is like an essay with a paragraph on each of several selected primary duties and attributes. The selected paragraphs could include such topics as organization, computer, general office, scheduling/event planning, accounting/financial, communication, and team participation. Each paragraph should include a general description of the item being evaluated, followed by the evaluation with supporting evidence. Supporting evidence is an incident that proves the evaluation. Write a summary paragraph that is positive and includes praise. Even if much improvement is needed, there is a positive way to write it.

The next portion of this review format is for goals. If this is her first review, the goals you should be evaluating would be the ones you set when she was first hired. The secretary sets her own goals thereafter. The boss should review the goals with the secretary. There should be a place on the review form for the secretary to write her own evaluation of her goals. The format should include a final section for the secretary to provide a written response to the complete performance review.

The second performance review format is the most commonly used and lists each of the secretary's specific duties. The boss then writes a short evaluation statement with supporting evidence. The balance of the format is the same as the first with a summary paragraph, goal evaluation, and response section.

The written evaluation is only the first step in the performance review. In the next step the boss needs to conduct a performance review interview with the secretary. In this interview the boss provides the secretary with a copy of the written review and they discuss its contents. This meeting should begin by praising the secretary and end by praising the secretary, no matter what the contents are.

After the interview the secretary will add her written goal evaluation and response to the written review she received. She also needs to set goals that will cover the span of the next review period. This does not have to be done immediately, although it should be completed within a few days. The secretary should present the completed written review to you at your weekly meeting. At this time you would discuss her new goals and response. It should then be signed by both of you, with copies going to her and to her personnel file.

Writing a performance review is not an easy task given the criteria with which it should be accomplished. Keep in mind that if it is done correctly this can be an excellent tool for building a harmonious working relationship.

INDEX

A

acceptance 20
accounting 3, 10, 52, 60, 88, 93, 116
administrative 3, 8, 9, 10, 24, 52, 68, 75, 78, 88, 90, 91, 94, 113
advisor 1
agenda(s) 3, 32, 82, 83, 84, 85
appointment 49, 50, 51, 52, 101
assignment(s) 14, 34, 36, 39, 40, 41, 43, 44, 45, 46, 47, 53, 54, 60, 76, 83, 84, 87, 88, 99, 105
assistant 1, 2, 8, 9, 10, 88, 90
attitude 1, 10, 11, 26, 28, 43, 53, 116
attributes 1, 3, 5, 6, 7, 10, 11, 35, 52, 91, 93, 94, 96, 114, 116

B

back rubbing 31
balance 22, 97, 117
bank 13, 14, 102
behavior 20, 30, 46, 80, 112, 114
birthday 24
blame 26, 28
bookkeeping 3, 5, 93
build(s) 12, 13, 16, 17, 39, 71, 103, 105, 111
building 12, 14, 22, 26, 28, 34, 88, 103, 117

C

calendar 2, 31, 37, 40, 41, 48, 49, 50, 51, 52, 53, 60, 69, 73, 93, 104, 105, 106
candidate 91, 94, 96
characteristic 93, 97, 98
Christmas 24, 100
client 56, 70, 73
command 9, 44, 47, 86
commitment 13, 38
committed 19, 20, 38, 74
communicate 16, 18, 19, 20, 50, 66
communication 3, 10, 13, 16, 18, 20, 34, 35, 38, 48, 59, 67, 68, 76, 77, 87, 88, 89, 94, 116
company 2, 28, 41, 49, 52, 53, 56, 59, 62, 67, 69, 70, 71, 72, 73, 76, 77, 78, 82, 87, 103, 104
compatibility 97, 98, 99
compliment 13, 14, 15, 97, 105, 106
composition 10, 13, 62, 77, 93
computer 2, 6, 18, 49, 52, 65, 76, 100, 103, 104, 107, 108, 109, 110, 116
condemnation 26
confidante 1, 20
confidentiality 3, 10, 20, 35, 94
conversation 18, 20, 39, 40, 57, 71, 87
converse 22
coordinating 2, 35, 48, 52, 83
correspondence 3, 10, 45, 56, 60, 62, 63, 64, 66, 70, 72, 73, 77, 78, 79, 80, 82, 102
courtesy 35, 46, 87, 112
CPS 9, 91
credibility 16, 42, 53, 82, 113
criticism 14, 26, 27, 29, 115
criticize 26
customer 52, 66, 69, 70, 79, 103

D

daily planner 40, 49, 53, 69
deadline 28, 49, 83, 99
dedicated 13, 90
defense 20
delegate 72, 87
destructive 26
devoted 42
dictation 2, 5, 55, 56, 57, 59, 92, 93
diplomacy 70, 71
direction 13, 16, 39, 53, 82, 105, 114

Index

disapproval 26
disrespect 24
document 2, 3, 6, 9, 10, 11, 18, 34, 35, 36, 45, 46, 57, 59, 61, 62, 63, 65, 66, 73, 76, 77, 78, 79, 82, 101, 104, 106
domino effect 53
down-time 36
draft 55, 56, 57, 62, 63, 73, 74, 79, 80, 81, 84
duties 1, 2, 5, 8, 9, 11, 13, 34, 35, 67, 70, 86, 100, 104, 106, 113, 116, 117
duty 11, 52, 69, 73, 75, 87, 116

E

edit 80, 84
editing 62, 79, 80, 81, 93
education 5, 9, 62, 91, 94, 96
electronic mail 93
email 3, 6, 18, 31, 34, 41, 46, 64, 74, 75, 76, 77, 103
encourage 26, 109, 110
encouraging 33, 115, 116
English 3, 6, 9, 61
environment 4, 12, 22, 35, 36, 49, 52, 60, 66, 97, 107, 115
ergonomic 107, 109, 110
error(s) 24, 26, 36, 45, 61, 69, 80
etiquette 3, 24, 60, 92, 94
evaluate 36, 37, 41, 92, 97, 99, 116
evaluation 28, 96, 116, 117
event 22, 39, 40, 41, 49, 52, 53, 54, 106, 115
event planning 10, 48, 52, 53, 54, 93, 116
executive 2, 8, 9, 10, 49, 50, 55, 90
expense 24, 56, 82, 100
experience 6, 9, 91, 92, 94, 96
expert 45, 61, 92

F

faultfinding 26, 80
feedback 114
file 6, 9, 34, 36, 45, 46, 56, 59, 60, 65, 66, 67, 72, 73, 85, 117
filing 2, 3, 5, 35, 64, 65, 67, 78, 102, 104
financial 10, 52, 88, 93, 116

G

gift 24, 100
goal 1, 2, 3, 13, 32, 34, 94, 106, 116, 117
grabbing 31
grammar 4, 9, 92

H

habit 35, 63, 97, 102
handshake 31
hardship 86
harmonious 12, 13, 28, 87, 100, 111, 117
hazardous 107
hear 20, 21, 42
hearing 20, 21
hire 16, 90, 91, 93, 96, 100, 102, 116
hiring 96, 97, 100
holiday 100, 106
honor 13, 24
honorable 31
humor 13, 22, 24, 25

I

imperfect 28
improvement 26, 115, 116
in-basket 34, 66, 74
influence 26, 89, 112
insensitivity 86
instructions 18, 34, 43, 45, 46, 50, 55, 57, 58, 69, 74, 75, 104
Internet 31
interruption 28, 36, 69
intuition 7, 53
intuitive 20

K

keyboard 2, 109, 110

L

labor law 96, 108
lead 53, 116
leader 28, 112, 113

119

leadership 94
Leading 113, 114
leading 114
letter 6, 31, 56, 58, 60, 61, 72, 77, 78, 79
level 2, 3, 8, 9, 10, 16, 24, 34, 39, 41, 44, 45, 49, 52, 55, 59, 60, 68, 69, 71, 72, 73, 75, 82, 88, 90, 91, 92, 93, 96, 104, 108, 110, 111, 113, 114
liaison 2, 49
life cycle 54, 73, 106
listen 20, 21, 39, 44
listening 13, 20, 21, 99, 114
loyal 13, 112
loyalty 22, 38, 112
lunch 24, 99, 101, 104, 108

M

mail 2, 16, 34, 44, 46, 58, 64, 68, 71, 72, 73, 74, 79, 92, 93, 102, 104
manual dictation 92, 93
meeting(s) 3, 18, 37, 38, 39, 40, 42, 46, 47, 49, 50, 51, 52, 64, 69, 71, 75, 82, 83, 85, 105, 106, 117
meeting minutes 82, 83, 84, 85, 93
memo 6, 18, 31, 79
memorandum 3, 56, 77, 78, 82
memories 7

memory 2, 6
message 18, 34, 41, 68, 75, 76
microcassette 2, 55, 56, 57, 79
micromanager 53
micromanaging 113
mission 31, 32
mistakes 22, 26, 28
music 99

N

negative 8, 13, 14, 20, 22, 26, 28, 46, 80, 97, 116

O

obstacle 28
offensive 30, 31
office personnel 35, 41, 86, 88, 89
office politics 86, 89
opinion 22, 39
organizational 3, 7, 10, 94, 116
out-basket 34, 46, 74

P

patting 31
performance review 47, 106, 115, 116, 117
perks 100, 101
persuasion 112
phone 2, 3, 9, 11, 18, 36, 41, 45, 46, 49, 50, 59, 68, 69, 74, 77, 79, 92, 103, 106
physical contact 31
pinching 31

positive 11, 22, 46, 94, 97, 112, 116
praise 13, 14, 15, 33, 102, 116
praising 117
present 2, 28, 34, 36, 41, 43, 45, 47, 50, 53, 74, 75, 115, 117
presentation 3, 10, 59, 60, 66, 75, 93
presenting 44, 46, 47, 59, 78
print 9, 32, 45, 48, 49, 51, 57, 60, 61, 62, 63, 71, 75, 77, 79, 81, 85
printing 51, 63, 80, 81
priority 18, 41, 44, 46, 57
problem 3, 28, 35, 56, 82, 94, 108, 115
procedure 5, 45, 51, 63, 64, 69, 76, 82, 83, 102, 106, 114
production 6, 10, 11, 34, 36, 59, 60, 61, 62, 63, 78
productive 3, 4, 13, 26, 36, 37, 42, 46, 71, 82, 98, 106, 112
profanity 29, 30
profession 1, 33, 91
professional 3, 4, 9, 31, 64, 68, 69, 71, 77, 91
professionalism 59, 60, 91, 94
project 22, 36, 41, 43, 44, 45, 53, 54, 56, 105

Index

proofreading 62, 79, 93, 80, 81
protocol 3, 67, 74, 76, 105
proverb 14, 16, 20, 22, 30, 63, 90
punctuation 4, 9, 61

R

radiation 107, 108
rapport 42, 89
real-time 44, 45
receptionist 9, 11, 68, 69, 87, 91, 104, 113, 114
reprimand 14
reprove 115
reproving 14, 102
respect 14, 16, 17, 24, 28, 31, 35, 38, 46, 51, 112, 113
respectful 16, 52, 78, 82
review 6, 10, 28, 39, 40, 41, 47, 63, 66, 69, 72, 74, 75, 76, 81, 94, 103, 104, 106, 115, 116, 117
reviewing 34, 74, 104

S

salaries 8, 82, 91
salary 8, 9, 10, 11, 90, 91, 92, 94, 100
schedule 14, 33, 36, 40, 47, 48, 51, 90, 101, 105, 114
Secretary's Day 24, 100
seminar 49, 52, 61
sexual harassment 30, 31
share 13, 16, 18, 42, 63, 67, 76, 89, 104
sharing 16, 18, 38, 42
shorthand 5, 55
skills 3, 6, 7, 10, 11, 45, 52, 68, 70, 92, 93, 94, 96, 113, 114
software 3, 44, 45, 60, 76, 92, 93, 94
spelling 4, 61, 80, 92
spreadsheet 3, 10, 60, 93
standard 45, 51, 60, 63, 64, 65, 67, 69, 77, 78, 80, 102, 114
style 48, 53, 56, 59, 60, 62, 77, 78, 80, 82, 92, 102, 104
supervise 113
supervising 112, 113, 114
supervisor 12, 39, 46, 76, 113

T

teacher 113, 114
teaching 113
team 1, 18, 32, 38, 54, 112, 113, 116
team effort 82
team player 3, 10, 94
telephone 2, 11, 16, 35, 36, 42, 50, 57, 64, 67, 68, 70, 92, 102, 103, 104, 105
thermostat wars 89
title 8, 9, 10, 11, 16, 30, 47, 76, 87, 88, 90, 91, 93, 102
to-do 34, 37, 41
tool 12, 13, 22, 28, 33, 45, 47, 48, 59,
76, 84, 111, 112, 114, 115, 117
train 102, 103, 113
training 49, 52, 103, 113, 114
transcribing 6, 10, 56
transcription 2, 93
travel 49, 52
traveling 101
trust 13, 26, 112
trusting 71, 103
trustworthy 13
typing 2, 56, 92, 93, 94
typist 1, 8

U

understanding 13, 28, 114
unimportant 42
urgency 44

V

vacation 49
vendor 52, 70, 76, 103
verbal 14, 30, 67, 75, 77
verbally 3, 16, 43, 76
visitor 3, 35, 36, 52, 64, 70, 71, 87

W

wardrobe 71
well being 13, 39, 112
workflow 33, 36, 38, 39, 47, 48, 67, 76, 79, 89, 105, 106

121